D0340293

*Assumptions of
Social Psychology*

Century Psychology Series

Richard M. Elliott, Kenneth MacCorquodale,
Gardner Lindzey, and Kenneth E. Clark
Editors

Robert E. Lana
Temple University

Assumptions of Social Psychology

New York

Appleton-Century-Crofts
Educational Division
Meredith Corporation

PRINTED IN THE UNITED STATES OF AMERICA

390-53800-0

to Jean

&

my mother and father

Preface

Between the physical scientist, focused upon inanimate objects, and the writer of fiction, concerned with human beings, is the psychologist, the Prometheus who would bring the method of the one to the subject matter of the other. In undertaking such a momentous task he must, like Prometheus, expect to have his liver picked over. It is inevitable that he will earn the epithets "addle-headed" from the scientist and "despicable" from the artist. Unfortunately, because of the inherent difficulty of the task and also his own reluctance to recognize the simplest conditions at the limits of given theories, the results of the psychologist's efforts during the past 150 years have hardly been Promethean. A major obstruction that has been acknowledged periodically throughout the history of psychology is the hesitation before or disregard of the changing nature of explanation at the frontiers of a particular subject matter. Thus, in areas such as the study of the higher mental processes, personality formation and change, and group behavior, the logical and empirical assumptions of explanatory systems, which are observationally based, have rarely been examined to determine both their limits and their possibilities. Establishing these limits and possibilities is crucial for the future of any system and for its successful use at the time of its most extensive acceptance by theorists. For example, it seems clear that the attempt at rapport between psychoanalysts and more experimentally oriented theorists suffers because the former regard the experiment as irrelevant within the psychoanalytic framework, whereas the latter consider prediction to be the ultimate criterion for understanding in any system of explanation. The two positions may be fundamentally incompatible, but, if so, we must know exactly where the incompatibility lies. In many instances conflict among various theoretical positions is logical in nature and represents irreconcilable interpretations of the nature of human beings. These difficulties are acute in areas such as the complex social processes, including creativity, love, and, in many cases, aesthetics.

One of the drawbacks (or perhaps it is an asset) of writing a book of this sort is that the author has difficulty deciding where it might successfully be used within the academic setting. I believe that the kinds of problems this book discusses should be introduced either simultaneously with or just after those of a more empirical nature usually included in the first course in social psychology. However, I also know that even the minimal degree of philosophical sophistication needed to follow the first chapters of this book is often lacking in sophomores who usually enroll in the first course in social psychology. Therefore, I expect that this book will be more useful for advanced undergraduate courses in social psychological theory and for similar courses at the graduate level. As for its helpfulness to my colleagues, only they can decide.

I am very much indebted for assistance and advice in writing the Hume-Kant chapter to two men whose help I consider indispensable. Stephen Mousouris was particularly helpful with the Kant section and most of the words in that section are his own. Eli Schutts was equally helpful in criticizing and commenting on the Hume section. Should this chapter be successful it is due to the efforts of these two men.

Merle Turner read the entire manuscript, and his comments were extremely helpful.

For grammatical correction of the manuscript and for extensive typing and rewriting, I am indebted to Jean Lana who performed these most tedious tasks without complaint.

I would also like to thank the students in my seminar at the Institute of Philosophy of the University of Rome for their comments and good sense and for their patience with some of the less well formulated ideas that constituted the initial draft of this book.

Rome, Italy   R. E. L.

Contents

ix

Contents

Introduction

Theories of psychology, like all others, are designed to provide what we may call an explanatory context from which specific data may be predicted. Social psychology in particular is concerned with providing this explanatory context for forms of activity that result from the interaction among human beings. An occasion of interaction involves two or more individuals who share a set of experiences; that is, they respond in a similar manner to similar stimuli provided by one another. Since the stimuli are almost invariably of a symbolic nature, this interaction is generally referred to as communication. In American psychology the term "social behavior" is quite often used to denote any form of response two or more people make to stimulation provided by one another. In this book, because certain distinctions are made between traditional behaviorism and other theoretical positions, we shall utilize "social activity" to denote these forms of social responses and save "social behavior" as a label for that type of "social activity" described by social psychological theories deriving specifically from behaviorism. A social psychological theory may have as its fundamental unit of study either a portion of activity gleaned directly from the shared experience or the activity to which this shared experience may be reduced.

1

The early chapters of this book will be devoted to an inquiry into the development of two fundamental ways of thinking about social phenomena. This will necessitate an examination of the concept of causality in its modern form, beginning with the work of Hume and Kant and continuing to the present day. The concepts of causality of these two contemporaneous philosophers contain, in germinal form, the two major approaches to understanding human social phenomena. I believe that many of the assumptive bases of the principal types of modern social psychological theories are grounded in one or the other of these two concepts of causality, and that this partly sets the tone for the further development of the modern theories and determines, again in part, the choice of empirical area to be emphasized by the theorist. This book makes no pretensions toward a complete history or analysis of assumptions preceding theory. Obviously, one can approach a study of the assumptions of social psychology from any number of points of view. The nature of and distinctions between quantitative and qualitative data, sheer classification and description, and the relationship between data and theory, all have their place as important scientific pre-problems. The decision to consider the assumptions rooted in causality is based on the belief that they are of paramount importance for understanding the widest context into which any psychological theory fits. An application of the conclusions reached here to noncausal statements may not be possible. However, wherever prediction of a future event is used as a criterion for the success of a given system of explanation, I believe the analysis made here will be relevant.

It is appropriate that a word be said about the connection between the concept of causality and the process of scientific theorizing. It seems clear that thinking about causality precedes the enterprise of science in general and psychology in particular. Description does play a role in theorizing, but it is always of an *ex post facto* nature, and is merely historical unless linked with prediction. Certainly in modern times the predictability of phenomena has been taken as the most important criterion of scientific success. Since most definitions of causality involve a two-part process (usually labeled cause and effect), in which the first event (cause) is given and the second event (effect) either follows closely in time or occurs simultaneously with the first, the prediction of the second event from the first arises as one kind of criterion for the success of an empirically based statement. However, prediction is not the totality of theory. We shall deal with this more thoroughly in the next three chapters. For the present it will be sufficient merely to point out that the actual propositions of any theory have a logical existence of their own and are not reducible to the empirical referents of the system, which referents form the basis for prediction. Yet, although the structure of a theory must be partly developed by processes which are independent of any empirical referents (and therefore independent of prediction), in order to test the credibility and usefulness of the theory one must ultimately depend upon prediction and therefore upon empirical referents.

We must now distinguish between two aspects of causality which are inherent in the usual use of the term. To do this I shall borrow from Bunge's (1959) separation of the concept of causation from that of causal principle. Causation refers to the causal connection in general, as well as to any particular causal connection or nexus. Thus, the statement "a thrown baseball produced the broken window" involves the process of causation. The causal principle refers to the law of causation where the invariance of the elements pertinent to causation is assumed. Thus, the statement "baseballs thrown swiftly against windows invariably break them," is an example of a causal law involving the causal principle. In most cases I shall use the term "causality" or "cause and effect" to mean both processes described above. In a good part of the discussion a discrimination between these two processes is not necessary. In other situations I believe it will be clear to which aspect of causality I am referring.

It may be useful to define one other term at this point. Again borrowing from Bunge, "determinism" or the "principle of determination" refers to the ontological position which holds that nothing may arise from nothing or pass into nothing, and that nothing occurs in an irregular, lawless manner. That is, "everything is determined in accordance with laws by something else," these being the internal and external conditions of the object or event in question (Bunge, 1959, p. 26, 1.7).

A concept we must take into account which is related to the concept of causality is that of reduction. There are at least two ways in which the term is used within the context of scientific theory. The first is when the microterms of one theory become the macroterms of another theory, the latter labeled the higher-level theory of the two. In this case, we say that the first theory has been reduced to the other if there is no excess meaning remaining in the first (reduced) theory. The second way refers to the general process of assuming, and sometimes demonstrating, that an observable process (such as learning to type) is analyzable in terms of another observable process (occurring, for example, in the central nervous system), such that one could explain the one from a preknowledge of the other, the learned performance from a preknowledge of the nervous activity. It may occur to the reader that both ways of describing reduction may be the same. For our purposes, it is necessary to draw a rather sharp distinction between actually observable data and the process of theorizing.

The first kind of reduction is accomplished when a theory, for example, in psychology, borrows a form or model from another discipline, for example, physics, in order to explain entirely different phenomena. The gestalt theorists have engaged in just such an attempt, and this will be discussed in Chapter Five. On the other hand, it is possible to maintain that motives and emotions in individuals are composed entirely of moving particles, and that if we understand the relations existing among elements of the latter we can understand and predict relations existing among elements of the former. Gestalt theorists, however, do not hold this latter position, and I believe the two possibilities are logically separable. Unless otherwise specified, when the term "reduction" is used, reference will be to reduction of one theory or theoretical term in a given system to a term or terms in another, rather than to the reduction of observed entities to other observed entities. In any case, I wish to avoid engaging in a polemic concerning the logical isomorphism, or lack of it, existing between the two types of reduction. Whatever their logical status, the discussions involving reduction in the text are not affected.

In Chapter One, the concepts of causality contained in the principal work of Hume (*A Treatise on Human Understanding*) and of

Kant (*The Critique of Pure Reason*) are summarized and discussed briefly. The current status of thinking about causality is dealt with in Chapter Two, with special attention paid to the work of Bertrand Russell and R. B. Braithwaite. In Chapter Three some related philosophical problems associated with the subject matter of psychology and the treatment of these problems by Ernst Mach are noted.

The remainder of the book is an attempt to make explicit the assumptions regarding the nature of the human organism, especially those concerning social phenomena, and the nature of theory used to explain these phenomena. The modern positions examined will be those with a predominantly psychological orientation, produced largely by experimental and social psychologists who are sophisticated in theory formalization and in the experimental process. In Chapters Four through Seven some modern social psychological theories are scrutinized in terms of their assumptive bases. The theories are very roughly divided into two groups: those with an essentially functional nature, historically derivable from behaviorism, such as the systems of B. F. Skinner, H. Helson, and others; and those derivable from gestalt theory, including the social theories of Kurt Lewin, Solomon Asch, Krech and Crutchfield, and T. Newcomb. Separate chapters are devoted to the social thinking of Freud and Horney, and to the theory of cognitive dissonance of Leon Festinger.

It is obvious that in the list of social psychological theorists just presented many well-known and successful individuals have been omitted. Since my purpose is to examine the *kinds* of assumptions made by various types of theories in social psychology, I believe it is justifiable to select those theories that best illustrate some of the diversity in this area. Some of those listed, such as Skinner and Helson, are not generally thought to be social psychologists. The inclusion of Skinner is necessary for at least two reasons. First, his system is particularly pure in terms of its adherence to a simple functionalism derivable from certain emphases made by Hume, Mach, and their followers. Second, he is one of the few modern theorists to attempt to explain, within a single system, behavior as diverse as that associated with simple conditioning and that associated with the creative process, thinking, and complex forms of social activity. Helson is included for similar reasons.

Since methodology is inseparable from the assumptions of any empirically based theory, some attention must be paid to the special problems that arise in the performance of experiments. Chapter Eight is a discussion of methodology and its relation to theoretical assumptions within social psychology.

The final chapter includes a summary, a further consideration of some of the conclusions reached in the earlier chapters, and a discussion of some emerging problems; for example, those involved with the attempt to explain creativity and the nature of fictional literature.

Comments on Some Aspects of the History of the Concept of Causality

Before beginning our discussion of Hume and Kant, it will be fruitful to glance for a moment at two of the principal figures who precede them in the historical development of the concept of causality. Aristotle was the first to deal with the concept in an extensive, systematic manner. Galileo's idea of causality was more consistent with the objective, scientific emphasis of the post-Renaissance. Following this, we shall introduce two modern conceptions of causality which are frequently used, that is, causality as constant conjunction and as necessary production. It is not necessary to consider theories of causality which are not directly relevant to the scientific process. For example, since Hegel believes the structure of the knowable world to be logical in nature, causality for him consists in the logical structure of various elements used to duplicate or reconstruct the causal connection in thought. Causality within the history of science is not used or defined in this sense, since no assumption is ever made within the scientific context that the structure of the world is knowable solely or principally through the application of logic.

Aristotle

Aristotle (1930) divided the process of causality into four identifiable types of cause. First is the material cause, which refers to the passive substratum out of which a theory comes to be and which persists. The second is the formal cause, which describes the ultimate nature of the thing, that is, the statement of the archetype or essence, usually given by a mathematical relation of some sort. Third is the efficient cause, which indicates the source of motion involving an external compulsion affecting a body in the most general sense; for example, the father is the cause of the child, and the sun is the cause of heat, etc. The fourth cause is the final cause, which specifies the end or purpose or "good" of anything. Although scientists dating from the Renaissance concentrated upon Aristotle's efficient cause as most relevant to their efforts, we may add the formal cause as relevant to recent efforts at understanding the total process of causality, and dismiss, for our purposes, the first and fourth causes. Aristotle's formal and efficient causes are both relevant to the idea of constant conjunction as well as to that of productivity.

Since the efficient cause referred to an extrinsic motive force which produced an effect, it is relatively simple to associate this two-part process with the observation of discernible events and thus to ground the entire enterprise in the initial procedures of empirical science. This, of course, is just what happened during the Renaissance when intense interest in observation of nature began.

The formal cause of Aristotle has become part of the modern conception of scientific theory and is still maintained as a property of theory construction which is distinctly separate from the efficient cause associated with observation. We shall continue our discussion later in Chapter Three under the rubric of theory construction and of the constant conjunction interpretation of cause.

Galileo

In the early post-Renaissance days, Galileo supplied the scientific world with a definition of causality which is both simple and workable. Efficient cause is defined as the necessary and sufficient condition for the appearance of an object or event. The presence of a cause is always followed by its effect, which is produced by no other than that cause. When the cause is removed, the effect disappears. Without dealing with some of the difficulties of this definition, we see that it represents a more concrete, practical conception of the process of causality than the definitions offered by Aristotle. Galileo's definition allows for a focus upon the empirical determinants of a given effect, such that the removal of a cause allows for an immediate test of its status by observing whether its attendant effect also disappears. However, the definition lacks specificity in determining the cause, since any event producing the effect may be labeled the cause of it and we have little more than a system of classification of certain classes of contiguous events. Also, what it gains in immediate usefulness over the Aristotelian definitions, it loses in restriction to a particular epistemology and ontology which involves less of the total scientific process of causation and theorizing than do the Aristotelian concepts. Modern science has returned to some of the old Aristotelian concerns, away from the stricter, more definite conceptions of Galileo and those following him. This is not to say that Galileo failed to perceive the problem as well as Aristotle. On the contrary, Galileo's conception of causation was a decided step towards a then necessary practical specification of fundamental scientific procedure. He was the first great theoretician of science, as well as the leading practicing scientist of his day. And it was his kind of thinking which led to what are perhaps the two most modern interpretations of the nature of causality within the scientific enterprise.

Causality as Constant Conjunction

This point of view is exemplified by the proposition, "If C then (and only then) E always." This kind of formulation does not allow us to make a distinction between propositions of the types, (1) "Continually administered erratic punishment causes neurosis," and (2) "Hooded rats have better visual acuity than albino rats." The first statement is directly causal and the second asserts a correlation between two qualities. The statements are not intended to convey the same kind of relationship in the usual way they are used, yet both "fit" the definition of causality as constant conjunction. In some of the theoretical orientations within psychology (for example, that of Skinner) it is not important to make this distinction. A causal conception based on constant conjunction of the cause with the effect is not only suitable but desirable. It states only a simple relationship among events. It makes possible a conservative set of empirically based conclusions. Error is less likely than when the definition of cause includes more elements (for example, production). However, for reasons which will be given in Chapters One, Two, and Three, this formulation of the idea of causality is inadequate for all but a limited kind of scientific thinking.

Causality as Necessary Production

A definition of causality which adds the ingredients missing from the constant conjunction interpretation must include the category of connection; that is, a reference to things being produced by other things. The following is an informal definition of this conception of causation given by Bunge: "If C happens, then (and only then) E is always produced by it" (1959, p. 47). The effect does not merely succeed the cause, or accompany it, it is brought forth by it. It is difficult to demonstrate that this really depicts what is happening within the framework of a given theory in a scientific discipline. This particular problem is discussed at some length in Chapter Two, in which the work of R. B. Braithwaite is introduced.

In the following chapter, most of the problems connected with the concept of causality will be discussed within the context of the causal theories of two of the outstanding epistemological and ontological thinkers of the eighteenth century, David Hume and Immanuel Kant, whose points of view remain the basis for modern psychological theorizing. The revolution in philosophical interpretations of causality begun by Hume, and the attempt at refutation and clarification by Kant, shed a great deal of light upon modern conceptions of scientific procedure and the general problem of determinism. I shall attempt to show that a psychological theorist's fundamental assumptions regarding man, and the process of theorizing about him, depend greatly upon his implicit or explicit view of the nature of causality and of determination. Beginning our discussion with Hume and Kant allows us as well to emphasize the centrality of cause, determination, empiricism, and holism in modern theories of social psychology.

part I

The Philosophical Basis

The first three chapters of this study will be concerned with Hume and Kant's concepts of cause and effect in themselves and as they culminate in R. B. Braithwaite's ideas about the nature of scientific explanation, especially those dealing with cause and effect, inference, and reduction. Chapter One deals with Hume and Kant's theories of causality, while Chapter Two extends this discussion to the contemporary work of Bertrand Russell and R. B. Braithwaite, who have supplied needed clarification and extension. Indeed, Russell and Braithwaite may have provided a solution to the problem of the existence and characteristics of the concept of necessity in the causal relation. We shall see that, although there appears to be no contradiction between Hume and Kant regarding causality, many philosophers and scientists who have been aware of the centrality of this concept in making inferences from empirical observations have acted as if there were a contradiction and, consequently, have built empirical systems in which essential differences in theoretical Weltanschauung did actually arise.

The work of Ernst Mach is introduced in Chapter Three. He was perhaps the first theorist to emphasize the notion of contingency in Hume's analysis while minimizing Hume's concern over his discovery that necessity appeared to play no role in the cause and effect relationship. Thus, it is through the work of Mach that we see the beginning of the functional-contingency emphasis which was to be made by many scientists and which culminated in the behaviorist tradition. In Chapter Three we shall also indicate the possibility that some aspects of the modern gestalt approach to psychology may have been derived from other ideas in Mach's thinking.

Mach and many of those who followed him distinguished between Hume's initial skepticism regarding cause and effect and Kant's emphasis on the *a priori*. We shall see that this distinction did not represent as wide a difference in those two thinkers as it appeared to Mach and to many modern theorists who chose to focus upon the difference between Hume's contingency analysis and Kant's *a priori* focus (where necessity is introduced by the characteristics of the causal inferrer). Mach and later theorists tended to submerge Hume's concern with necessity in the cause and effect relationship and this eventuated in, among other developments, the modern American behaviorist stand on what constituted the basic process of scientific inference from observed instances. Other theorists, impressed with Kant's attempt to explain where this necessity lay, pursued a course of inquiry that led to, among other things, modern gestalt psychology.

chapter

1

The Theories of Cause and Effect of Hume and Kant

Hume

For David Hume the problem of understanding the nature of the universe implied that man's nature must first be fully understood. His investigations in this area culminated in his monumental treatise on human nature (Hume, 1961). Hume's treatise is important for the development of the present book because it deals with man's cognitive processes and, consequently, with man's attempt to develop rules for gathering information about his own nature.

For Hume, the initial human experience is the impression, roughly equivalent to what a modern American psychologist might call a discriminatory response to some discernible stimulus configuration. It should be emphasized that Hume made no assumptions regarding the existence of external stimuli preceding the occurrence of an impression. From these impressions the individual derives simple ideas which exactly represent, and which are always preceded by, their corresponding impressions. Since similar ideas and impressions are in constant conjunction, he concludes that one may come to believe that there is a connection between our many ideas and impressions which cannot arise from chance and, therefore, that there

13

is a dependence as well. Thus, the perception of cause and effect is anchored in the psychological nature of the organism, although this would not establish the logical validity of that concept for Hume, as we shall see below.

Hume was more concerned with the nature of the relationship between two simple ideas than with that between an impression and an idea. Because ideas succeed one another rapidly in time in the experience of the individual, Hume believed that he needed to establish the basis for their connection. He used the concept of association of ideas to account for the connection between simple ideas. Were ideas loose and unconnected, chance alone would join them, but since they are not, the principles of association account for their joining. At this point one may understand that, since Hume believes that the cognitive processes contain the notion of cause and effect, the initial condition of causation necessary for the appearance of an idea is to be found in the psychological nature of the organism and not in an abstract principle or in an assumption of logic or of metaphysics. The modern interpretation of this unique anti-ontological (presuppositionless) explanation of cause and effect is somewhat different, but it is still largely influenced by Hume. As we shall see below, Kant's position on causation is also anti-ontological.

The three principles of association are resemblance, contiguity in time or place, and cause and effect. We need not dwell upon the condition of resemblance of ideas for the occurrence of association. Presumably, because of similar elements existing among ideas, the presence of one idea introduces or recalls another. So also for contiguity. Although my grandmother and her shawl do not particularly resemble one another, I have rarely seen one without the other and, hence, the presence of one calls up the idea of the other. The act of throwing a switch is associated with the idea of increased illumination following shortly after. The condition of cause and effect produced in the understanding by this event, and which, in turn, produces the association of ideas relevant to the event is, according to Hume, the most forceful of the three conditions. It is also the most complex and difficult to comprehend. The relation of father and son by blood is a causal relationship, notwithstanding resemblance and contiguity of the impressions or the ideas that derive from the relationship. Because words and ideas are so commonly connected, we use words for ideas, and the mind easily mistakes one for the other. Thus, the criterion of resemblance is often confused with the inferential idea of cause and effect.

Since the power by which one idea produces another idea is never discoverable by examination of either one or both of the ideas involved, it follows that cause and effect are relations of which we receive information from experience and not from abstract reasoning. Here then is the basic anti-ontological position maintained by Hume. It is a position well within the framework of the empiricist tradition to that time, depending as it does on the fact of experience to the exclusion of an abstract initial assumption. The peculiar relationship between Hume and Kant on this very point is worth exploring and will be discussed later.

When two objects are present to the senses and bear a certain relation to one another, e.g., one object appearing behind another object, this is called a perception and has nothing to do with reason. It is directly given and noninferential. The mind need not go beyond the perception to understand fully the relationship existing between the objects. Only the experience of causation allows the human understanding to go beyond the immediately given perception and produces the idea of necessary connection between two objects. From it, we are at least assured that the existence of one object was preceded or followed by the existence of another object. If from experience we observe the constant conjunction of two objects or their constant remoteness from one another, there is nothing in the objects themselves that allows us to conclude they are always this way. We do conclude that there is some as yet indiscernible cause which unites or separates them. Thus, of the three major relations involved in the association of ideas—resemblance, contiguity, and cause and effect—only cause and effect may involve processes beyond our senses.

Since the idea of cause and effect associated with two objects *is* an idea, it must have an impression or impressions which are prior to it. Clearly the impression cannot be found in any quality or characteristic of either of the two objects involved, since if found in one it may not be in the other. Also, a third object may have qualities completely unlike the first two and yet fall into a cause and effect sequence with them. The idea of causation, therefore, must be derived from some relation among objects.

The first characteristic discovered by Hume of the cause and effect relationship among objects is that of contiguity in space and time. Previously, the principle of contiguity of objects or actions was a separate characteristic. It contributed to the idea of association among objects but did not necessarily involve the idea of cause and effect. The issue is somewhat clouded here. Apparently simple ideas can be associated by means of contiguity in space or time without the idea of cause and effect being involved. However, the principal basis for the complex idea of cause and effect is that of contiguity in space and time. These are not contradictory statements as they stand, but the issue is further muddied if we consider that Hume conceived that all objects or actions could be either cause or effect. Hume's position is consistent in the following manner:

1. All objects can be either cause or effect.
2. Any two given objects in contiguity with one another in space and/or time often produce a simple idea of association but not necessarily one which involves the idea of cause and effect.
3. Two objects perceived in a cause and effect relation to one another are always contiguous in space and/or time.

When an event at some distance from another appears to be the cause of it, a chain of events and, hence, of causes and effects will most likely be found between the two observed objects. There is now cause and effect without contiguity between the two given objects. Although Hume ultimately rejects cause and effect as anything other than contiguity among events, the possibility of chains of cause and effect sequences made it possible for later thinkers to postpone the question of whether any two given events exist in a causal relation to one another. It is possible that some events may not partake of either the property of cause or of effect. One may simply beg the question by noting that the event is involved in causation through an as yet undiscovered causal chain containing other events. The position is irrefutable but, as we shall see below, sometimes unfruitful for understanding certain aspects of human behavior.

We have seen that, for Hume, the relation of contiguity is essential to causation. A second relation is that of the priority in time of the cause to the effect. We need not be detained by Hume's argument supporting this point. Since resolving the problem is not of central importance to the development of the theses of this book, it is sufficient to say that Kant comes to that same conclusion although Bertrand Russell does not.

At this point in his thinking, Hume makes the remarkable conclusion that he can discover no other relations which are relevant to the idea of causation. When Hume says that a cause produces an effect, he means that one event follows another event contiguously in space and time. Hume reduces the concept of production within the framework of causation to the notions of contiguity and priority in time. While denying the logical legitimacy of the classical concept of *production* (necessary connection) associated with cause and effect, Hume does assert that we have an *idea* of *necessary connection* between the cause and the effect since all objects exist in a relationship of contiguity and of priority with one another. Hume's principal argument against the idea that every event which has a beginning must have a cause is based on his observations of the impossibility of claiming an effect to be the production of a cause. The ideas of necessity and productivity are linked. Since it is denied that the concept of productivity is valid for a cause and effect relationship, the idea of necessity reduces to the notion of productivity and the argument against it is the same. He also argues that we can imagine a nonexistent entity for the first time without the principle of productivity or necessity being conjoined with this process. Without disturbing the principles of logic, it therefore can be assumed with equal facility that an event occurs with a cause and that it occurs without a cause.

Since the idea of necessary connection is neither derived from logical reasoning nor is directly observable, the question arises of how all individuals experience an idea of causation. Some sort of individual experience forces upon a person the notion of the necessity of an effect following its cause or the production of an effect by a cause. I might reason that if I move my arm in a certain fashion, I have caused the ball in my hand to be propelled into space at a certain rate. This experience allows me to presume that I have produced the motion in the ball by my preceding activity. Thus, the motion of the ball is necessarily produced by the cause which is my muscular activity, all according to the laws of motion.

According to Hume, all ideas concerning cause and effect must begin with impression on the part of the experiencing individual. Although one may conceive of causation in an abstract fashion, for example, as implied in Newton's first law, the initial experience from which the law has been formed was a sense impression involving specific objects. The initial idea of memory or impression of the senses necessary for the idea of cause and effect is unexplained and perhaps, for Hume, inexplicable. The origin of memory or impression is also taken as irrelevant for an understanding of the psychological nature of the concept of cause and effect. The initial idea in memory or impression, the necessary condition for the idea of causation, is given in a situation where two events are seen as contiguous in space and/or time. The prior event is perceived as cause. Since there is nothing about this sense impression which allows one to conclude that causation is present between the events, some process of inference from the impression of the contiguous events to the idea of cause and effect must be operating.

Since no event implies the existence of any other, as already has been established, it is only by experience that we can infer the existence of one event from another. We remember that in all past instances of observing one event, we have observed another event in temporal and spatial conjunction with it. Without further analysis, we proclaim the initial event cause and the second event effect. We add to the relations of contiguity and of succession the relation of constant conjunction, i.e., non-contradicted repetitions of the two events. Although surprised by his discovery that the essential ingredient of the idea of cause and effect was that of constant conjunction, Hume felt small satisfaction with his solution and believed it advanced understanding of causation but little. Hume, as would any other individual, felt compelled to believe in necessity between what he called cause and what he called effect. He believed that his temporary conclusion, that constant conjunction seemed the only objective element associated with causation, was unsatisfactory. Necessity seemed to be a common sense portion of the concept of causation, and yet he could not legitimately introduce it as a distinct, meaningful idea in his analysis. Later thinkers have partially resolved the problem in a manner which derives partially from Kant. The repetition of events in constant conjunction, no matter how many occurrences, provides no *reason* for concluding the necessity of one event following another. The idea of necessary connection cannot legitimately be inferred from the circumstance of repeated observations of the constant conjunction of two events. There is no principle of logic available that will allow us to conclude that instances of which we have no experience are similar to past instances of which we have memory. Therefore, the witnessing (many observations) of event B following event A closely in space and time generates no principle by which, upon the next appearance of A, we may legitimately expect the appearance of B soon afterward.

When necessity between cause and effect is eliminated by the argument that constant conjunction is the sole property by which an individual concludes that an effect has resulted from a cause, the concept of probability is introduced into the discussion. Probability is based upon ideas from impressions or memory or both. The modern investigation of the mathematics of probability has seen the extension and complication of an idea which remained comparatively simple for Hume. For him, probability was derived from the observation of past occurrences, and expectation of future occurrence based on that observation. Thus, ultimately, an inference from one event to another is based upon past experience. For although there is no process of logic by which we may legitimately conclude that an effect will follow a cause simply because we have often observed the event associated with cause to have preceded the event associated with effect, there is a tendency for all individuals to make this assumption. All reasoning based on probability and, hence, all reasoning from cause to effect, is based upon a kind of sensation. Hume had succeeded in reducing all reasoning from cause and effect to the conjunction of selected sensations. This is a very conservative way of making empirical inferences from various events. One is relieved of demonstrating the necessity of a particular observed effect following from a particular observed cause.

Hume's conception yields the following psychological proposition: If two events were, in the past, in constant conjunction and were contiguous in space and time, the mind would tend to produce the idea of one when the other was present to it. Since this cause and effect association seems to be a property of human thought, the only question that remains is whether or not it can be of any use for the individual in gaining knowledge about events which are formed into cause and effect associations. Kant reacts very strongly to this point, as we shall see later.

By means of cause and effect, one comes to belief. We have expectations of occurrences, and believe they will happen in the future under certain conditions, because we have had the psychological, as opposed to logical, experience of the constant conjunction of two events in time and/or space in the past. Man's reasoning is thus derived from sensation, that is, experience, and association or habit. Hume agrees that it appears quite ridiculous to say that it is only probable that all men must die or that the sun will rise tomorrow, although one has no possibility of affirming this consequence other than that provided by previous experience. He attempts to solve the problem created by his own investigations by separating the ideas of probability and of cause and effect into two kinds. He then makes a vague and unsatisfactory distinction between statements arising from relations of cause and effect that are free from uncertainty (such as the sun rising in the morning), and those from relations of cause and effect that are still attended with uncertainty. Both of these situations result in probability statements which have the same epistemological status and, therefore, the distinction is useless for solving the problem of accounting for necessity in causation.

In discussing the relation between cause and effect and necessary connection, the argument yields one conclusion which is of startling significance. Since any idea arises from an impression, the idea of necessity therefore must arise from some impression. However, Hume also demonstrates that there is no impression which can give rise to the legitimate idea of necessity in the external world; therefore, the only possible explanation remaining is that the psychological *propensity* in the individual which habituates him to pass from the impression of one object to *the idea of the object* is the condition which yields the idea of necessity. The important implication in Hume's discovery is that the idea of necessity may be part of the native understanding that the mind of the individual brings to a cause and effect situation. Hume anticipates Kant here. He has made a conceptually illuminating start to the solution of the problem of necessity.

In summary, the following can be said about Hume's ideas concerning the nature of cause and effect:

1. The cause and effect are contiguous in space and time.
2. The cause is prior to the effect.
3. There is a constant conjunction or union between the cause and the effect.

A major continuation of Hume's analysis of the nature of causation is found in the work of Immanuel Kant, to which we now turn.

Kant

When it is understood that Kant's *Critique of Pure Reason* (1961) was written partly in reaction to the work of David Hume, one may begin to comprehend the close association of modern views on the nature of man which developed from the ideas of these two men. The problem for both thinkers was how man proceeded to understand himself and the world around him. Hume and Kant are not in such opposition as might be expected from a reading of some of the secondary sources (e.g., Boring, 1950) widely used by psychologists. However, to minimize their very real epistemological differences would be unfruitful for understanding the assumptions of modern social psychology. In the next chapter, it will be shown how behavioral scientists in the main followed the epistemological lead of Hume, while phenomenological scientists found Kant's thesis more compatible with their own concepts.

We may begin our discussion of Kant by pointing out the difference between analytic and synthetic statements. In all statements where there is a relation between subject and predicate (e.g., affirmative statements), either the concept *B* belongs to the subject *A,* or *B* lies outside the sphere of influence of *A.* In the first instance, Kant calls the relationship "analytical" and in the second, "synthetic." Analytic statements involve a predicate which is contained in the idea of the subject, whereas synthetic statements add something to the idea of the subject by the pronouncement of the predicate. Kant cites the statement, "all bodies are extended," as an example of analytic judgment, and "all bodies are heavy" as an example of synthetic judgment. Since analytic statements serve only to clarify existing knowledge and do not add to it in any way, synthetic statements are usually of greater importance.

Both Hume and Kant take brute experience as the starting point of their epistemologies. But the fundamental units of that experience are quite different for each thinker. For Hume they are impressions and ideas; and for Kant the fundamental units are the act of synthesis and the given manifold. Kant's problem in following Hume was that he was convinced that the principle of causality is neither self-evident nor capable of logical demonstration. Either Hume's sceptical conclusions must be accepted, or we must be able to point to some criterion which is not dependent on experience but on which experience itself is dependent.

In each of its momentary phases experience can be analyzed into an endlessly variable material called the manifold, which comprises the contents of sensation, and into a fixed set of interdependent relational elements which are the forms of sensibility (called "forms of intuition" by Kant), the categories of the understanding, and the ideas of reason. As these relational elements are synthetic (Hume's influence makes itself felt here), they can be established only as essential conditions of our sense experience. As these relational elements are absolutely necessary for the structuring of our experience, they are *a priori*. *A priori* to Kant is both a necessary and a relative concept, necessary in that human experience has this particular structure, and relative in that human experience of the world is not an experience of the world as it is in itself, but as it is necessarily-for-us. The *a priori* relational elements are therefore as strictly factual as the experiences which they structure.

Kant proposes three levels of reality:

1. An ultimate reality (called "things-in-themselves" or "noumena") which transcends and generates human experience but is unknowable.
2. A realm of appearances (the phenomenal world) which is the objective, experienced world *common* to all *human* conciousness but not reducible to the merely subjective states of individual human beings.
3. A realm of purely private imaginings.

The irreducible relational elements in the objective, experienced world, as mentioned above, are the forms of sensibility, the categories of the understanding, and the ideas of reason.

The forms of sensibility are space and time. These are pure forms of perception which are not generated by empirical perceptions, but in fact are presupposed by them. Since sensations differ only qualitatively (a basic Kantian assumption), the form of space must be added by the mind, producing "side-by-sideness" and extension of objects. Space must be a necessary representation *a priori,* for it is impossible even to imagine the absence of space, although it is perfectly possible to imagine space as existing without objects to fill it. Since space cannot be "thought away" or "perceived away," it must be *a priori,* that is, a necessary relation of appearances to one another in the common world of appearance.

The *a priori* aspect of time is demonstrated in much the same manner, although time does not determine the relation of appearances to one another, but only the relation of representations in our inner state. The idea of time does not originate in, but is presupposed by, the senses. When a number of things act upon the senses, it is only by means of the idea of time that they can be represented as simultaneous or as successive. The notion of time, even if acquired through experience, cannot adequately be defined as a series of actual things existing one after another. For one can only understand the meaning of "after" if he already knows what time means. Since time is an *a priori* relation, we cannot know whether or not it is a relation of things-in-themselves. Inner processes are not known with any greater certainty than are outer appearances.

The second set of irreducible relational elements is the twelve categories of the understanding. These are twelve intellectual forms which may be contrasted to the pure forms of sensibility discussed above. Certain pure concepts, or categories, originate in the understanding. These categories combine with the perceptual forms of sensibility and the variable manifold of sense-contents to produce the consciousness of an ordered experience. For our purposes, the most crucial of these categories is that of causality.

In order to demonstrate how the category of causality is necessarily presupposed in the consciousness of an ordered experience, Kant distinguishes between the consciousness of the merely subjective order of our apprehension and the consciousness of the objective flow of events. He gives two examples. If we apprehend a house by successively apprehending the different parts of it, there is no necessity to begin at the roof and then go to the basement. We could start at the basement and work our way up to the roof just as easily. We would not regard either of these sets of successive perceptions as representing anything characteristic of the house. On the other hand, if we see a ship gliding down a stream, our apprehension of its place higher up in the course of the stream must come first. It is impossible in the apprehension of this phenomenon that the ship should be perceived first below and then higher up. Here, the order in the succession of our apprehensions is determined and our apprehension regulated by that order. In the example of the house, there was no order in the succession of perceptions determining the point where we had to begin. While in the apprehension of the ship gliding downstream, the order of successive perceptions was necessary. We are compelled to apprehend the ship as going downstream. We cannot reverse at will the order and apprehend the ship going upstream as we can reverse at will the starting point of our perception of the house. In order to distinguish objective succession from subjective succession, we must regard the former as compelling to our perception; that is, in order to be apprehended as objective succession, it must be understood as necessitated by causal connections. The category of causality is a logical presupposition of the objective succession of events in time. All possible experience, that is, all objective knowledge of phenomena with regard to their relation in the succession of time, depends on the category of causality.

There are two misunderstandings we must avoid here. The first is that while Kant has so far limited the principle of causal connection of phenomena to their succession, he finds as a practical matter that it applies also to their coexistence, because cause and effect may exist at the same time. If we look upon a ball that rests on a soft cushion and makes a depression in it, we see a cause simultaneous with its effect. But we nevertheless distinguish the two. If we place the ball on a cushion, the cushion's smooth surface is followed by a depression, while if there is a depression in the cushion, a ball by no means follows from it. The *irreversible* sequence relation remains even if there is no interval between the two events. It is the irreversibility that is the decisive consideration.

In order to avoid the second misunderstanding, it is necessary to distinguish between the causal principle and specific causal judgments. We have been discussing the general principle that every event must have *some* cause in that which immediately precedes it. What in each instance this cause is can only be discovered empirically, and one can never be absolutely certain. Kant would agree with Hume that the sun need not rise tomorrow. If wax has melted, we know *a priori* that *something* must have preceded it (e.g., the heat of the sun), after which the melting has followed according to a law, although without experience we could not know *a priori* either the cause from the effect, or the effect from the cause. Kant would insist that Hume was wrong in inferring the contingency of the causal principle from the contingency of *specific* causal judgments. Although we cannot be sure what causes the wax to melt, it does not follow that something does not necessarily cause it to do so. The category of causality enables us to predict *a priori* that for every event there must be some pre-existing cause, but only through empirical research can we pinpoint the specific cause.

The third set of irreducible relational elements is the ideas of reason. The categories of the understanding and of causality are limited to experience, for the categories are merely forms for relating phenomena and are in themselves empty. For instance, the attempt to prove the existence of God through the concept of causality would be impossible because it would be extending causality beyond experience. The principle of causality dictates that in our sensibility, that is, in space and time, every condition which we can reach in examining given phenomena is again conditioned. These phenomena are not objects by themselves in which something absolutely unconditioned might possibly exist. The categories place the data of perception into relation with one another in such a way that every phenomenon must necessarily be thought of as being conditioned by other phenomena. Every phenomenon has its conditions, which leads to an infinite regress. Reason, however, is unsatisfied with this infinite regress. It seeks to reach the unconditioned itself, the self-caused which contains in itself the conditions for all phenomena. The ideas of reason are mental representations of the unconditioned arising because reason is filled with a much higher craving than merely to discover phenomena and understand them as *our* experience. It is the object of reason to ascend from the conditioned synthesis to which the understanding is always restricted, to an unconditioned synthesis beyond the understanding. Pure reason never refers directly to objects, but to the concepts of objects framed by the understanding.

There are three ideas of pure reason: the unconditioned for the totality (1) of all phenomena of the inner sense, (2) of all phenomena of the outer sense, and (3) of all the conditioned in general. These are the ideas of the soul, of the world, and of God. We shall pick the idea of God as a paradigmatic case. The ideas of reason must not be viewed as objective realities. One can never prove the existence of God through logical reasoning, but the phenomena of the world *must* be viewed *as if* they derived their existence from a rational creator. The purpose of the idea of God is not to enable us to grasp the essence of such a God, but to allow methodological postulates which will lead us to a systematic unity of empirical knowledge. The postulates are interpreted as merely regulative of empirical inquiry, and can never run counter to experience. Reason which seeks completeness of explanation must always act in accordance with them. The idea of God is the methodological postulate of the rationality and uniformity of nature. It is a guide to inquiry and not an objective existent. Kant compares the ideas of reason to the illusion by which objects are seen behind the surface of a mirror, an illusion which is indispensable if we are to be able to see what lies behind our backs. Although the ideas of reason convey no knowledge *per se,* metaphysics is possible in an empirical form, consisting of speculative hypotheses concerning the facts of experience, keeping in mind that these "facts of experience" are phenomena and not noumena.

It is useful to emphasize that Kant is concerned with the conditions of perceptual truth. He never provided an answer to the question of the relationship between perceptual truth and the world of objects in themselves. For Kant, there is an objective order to sensible phenomena. This order may have no connection with the order of objects as it exists in itself. The objective order is known when it follows from the invocation of a rule which allows that order and none other in the perception of the individual.

By way of summary, it may be profitable to point out some of the salient features of Kant's idea of cause and effect, particularly the features relevant to later theoretical scientific thinking. For an event to be distinguished from a subjective series of sense apprehensions, it must be conceived to have been caused by another event. Thus, perceptual objectivity may be produced by cause and effect. Although Kant occasionally implied that one may apprehend objective events which are not causal in nature, he placed emphasis upon the causal objective event as fundamental to man's understanding. We need not be concerned here with the difficulties in trying to interpret Kant's position on the nature of all objective events. The temporal order of the events, causally linked, is the essence of the objective event. Kant sought the necessary and sufficient conditions which would allow objective perceptual truth to be apprehended by the perceiver. Unlike Hume, who stressed the psychological qualities of the conception, Kant attempted an epistemological argument for the validity of the objective idea of cause and effect. Kant's idea of objective apprehension begins with the notion that experience is translatable into sense perception only through epistemological considerations. Cause and effect as a principle is presupposed by all judgments about the world of fact.

There need be no essential contradiction between Hume and Kant on the nature of the principle of cause and effect. Kant attempted to supply an explanation of the nature of necessity in the causal sequence, while Hume, puzzled at his inability to discover such a principle, proceeded no further, and left us with the idea of the constant conjunction of events as the principal characteristic of causation.

Although we conclude that there is no essential contradiction between Hume and Kant as to the nature of the causal relation, theorists working after the 18th century often have implied that there were by stopping at the point where Hume became puzzled by the apparent absence of necessity in the causal relation. It became a simple matter to dichotomize Hume's and Kant's positions on this matter. We shall examine instances of this development in later chapters.

We now turn to the modern conception of causation as it evolved from the work of these two men, and then to a discussion of the influence on psychology of these views. We shall see that modern interpretations first focussed upon presumed differences between the thinkers on the nature of cause and effect, and eventually left the area of concern about causation altogether.

chapter

2

The Current Resolution

Although the idea of cause and effect remains central in a consideration of modern scientific inference, the general notion of determination preoccupies current philosophers of science to a greater degree than it did Hume and Kant. It is essential that we examine some current ideas about the nature of determination, particularly with reference to the ontological status of causation.

In his book *Causality* (1959) Bunge distinguishes among several ways of conceiving of determination. Some are minor; the others refer either to the concept of the constant conjunction of events, or to that of the production of one event by another. Although he further delineates causality as a notion separate from but related to determinism, we saw in the Introduction that causality may be subdivided into ideas involving the constant connection of events, and those involving the production of one event by another. Bunge seems to follow Kant in holding that any statement of connection, for example, Einstein's $E=mc^2$, is deterministic but not causal, in that mc^2 is not produced by E, but rather is contained in it. The general statement that flying bullets cause glass to break is, on the other hand, a productive, deterministic, causal notion. The distinction between the two is in many respects similar to Kant's distinction between analytic and synthetic statements. It is also true, however, that Bunge believes that production need not necessarily be causal in nature, but this point need not detain us. Statistical determinacy of the sort found in probability statements is also seen to be deterministic but acausal, since statistical statements do not include the idea of production or involve any uniqueness of connection of the events.

While we recognize that there are various possible conceptions of determinism and causality, the ideas of constant conjunction, uniqueness of the conjunction, and productivity remain the central notions associated with causal determinism or causation. It is important to add that constant conjunction, unique conjunction, and productivity refer to *kinds* or *classes* of causes and effects, so that it would not be necessary for the same objects and the same spatial relations to be produced in order to demonstrate a causal sequence. Scientific replication of causal connections would be impossible without this qualification.

To represent the most modern thinking about causation and other related ideas, I have chosen the analyses of Bertrand Russell and C. B. Braithwaite. Russell grasps the Humean/Kantian dilemma regarding causality and gives it relevance to problems in modern science. Braithwaite places Russell's solution in the context of scientific theory construction.

Russell defines causal law, and we may take it to be synonymous with our terms causation and cause and effect, as any general proposition by means of which it is possible to infer the existence of one object or event from the existence of another or several other objects or events. The objects and events are sense-data. Over successive applications of the causal law the specific objects and events will be different, but the relationship among them will remain the same. Hence, a certain relation among classes of objects is the essence of the causal law. In the causal statement, the temporal condition of the pertinent events or objects must be specified because the object or event from which another is inferred (cause) bears a specific time relation (either prior, antecedent, or simultaneous) to the object or event inferred (effect). This contiguity among the relevant events leads the organism to expect certain results specifically because of it. The expectation is similar to that mentioned by Hume in his psychological analysis of the causal inference natural to all individuals. Russell refers to the expectation as an "animal belief in causality," and notes that it can be observed in horses, dogs, etc. Although this kind of causal analysis usually results in identifying one event as cause and another as effect, the identification is more primitive than the idea contained in the concept causal law, which involves a statement of invariance, not merely an expectation of succession.

In the usual use of the terms "cause" and "effect," the cause is seen to be invariably prior to the effect, as Hume and Kant had it. However, the concept of causal law allows temporal priority neither to the events or objects identified with cause, nor to those identified with effect. There is no valid inference one may make with respect to expectations of future events based upon observed relevant contingencies in the past. That is, there is no characteristic of the contingency of events in the past which allows one to make the logical jump to expectation of events in the future, although, as has been pointed out by Hume and Russell, there is a psychological tendency to do so. If, however, a principle of induction (inferring an event from its past relationships with other events) is an *a priori* logical law, then the problem of providing logical justification for the psychological tendency to infer future events from past events is solved. The law would take the form of identifying future expectation with increasing probability of occurrence of one event following another, when the event has always followed the other event in the past. As the number of successful appearances of the relationship increases, the probability of the occurrence of the association of events approaches certainty. It is Russell's contention that it may be this principle of induction, rather than a principal of causality, which is fundamental to all inferences concerning objects or events not immediately given. Here Russell takes a unique position with respect to the nature of causality. It is a simple synthesis of reductive empiricism, which holds that the principles of logic are reducible to experiential associations, and of Kantian idealism, which holds that deductive logic is based upon *a priori* principles. It is to be emphasized that Russell is referring to induction and not to causality with respect to his presumed discovery of this *a priori* principle. However, since induction seems to lie at the base of causal laws for Russell, the two conceptions are really related. Perhaps we have here the beginning

of a solution to the Hume-Kant problem of locating necessity or production in the causal statement (causal law, in Russell's terms).

However, Russell's position on the *a priori* characteristics of induction changed radically from 1914, when he stated these views in
the Lowell Lectures of that year, to 1948, when he revised his stand.
In 1948, he stated categorically that induction is invalid as a logical
principle. His proof of this contention is simple. If all the elephants
I have seen are in India, perhaps I will conclude that all elephants
are in India. The fallacy in this argument is obvious, but there would
be no fallacy if induction by simple enumeration were a purely logical
principle. Hence, the *a priori* quality of causation can not be found
in the criterion of induction which characterizes part of it. The problem is to determine which, if any, *a priori* elements enter the inferential process, and where they do so.

In differentiating cause from causal law, Russell states that the
sense of the cause compelling or producing the effect, which most
people experience (including Kant and Hume), is invalid. We do
this because we associate cause with human volition. Yet, if there
were no legitimate way to infer the compelling aspect of cause with
respect to its effect, then the temporal order of cause and effect is
irrelevant to making a causal statement. Both the compelling aspect
of cause, and its priority in time to the effect, are usually derived
from the situation where a single object or event is observed as cause,
and another as effect. Within scientific reality there is usually a multiplicity of causes and effects involved in most statements of empirical
invariance, and this further reduces the illusion that a cause compels
its effect. Note that all ideas such as cause and effect, or causal law, or
law of causality, have no necessary *a priori* base. Whether or not any
law of causality remains valid with respect to any or all data would
demand further empirical observation, according to Russell.

In *Human Knowledge—Its Scope and Limits,* written in 1948,
which is perhaps his final word on the matter, Russell expands his
conception concerning cause and effect and induction. Since every
finite set of observations is explainable or predictable by several
mutually inconsistent laws, each having the same inductive evidence

in its favor, pure induction is invalid as the only criterion for the truth of scientific laws. This argument is a refutation of the oft-quoted position attributed to John Stuart Mill concerning criteria for the validity of scientific statements, and comes closer to one of Kant's fundamental points on the nature of inference. When induction seems to support a law, it turns out that the law has really been established in our thinking independent of any evidence cited to support it.

Causal Line

"Cause" means something different than "invariable antecedent." Two clocks in good running order both indicate three o'clock at the same time, but in no way do we suppose that the position of one set of hands has caused the position of the other set. Also, in most empirical observations antecedents are not invariable but only probable. Russell, disagreeing with Hume, begins from essentially the same point as did Kant. He will arrive at a different conclusion.

A "causal line" is a series of events whereby, if given some of them, we can infer something about the others, without having to know anything about their environment. When two events belong to the same causal line, the one prior in time may be called the "cause," and the antecedent one, the "effect." There is a certain validity to the statement *"A causes B"* if it is conceived in this manner. Because conceiving of cause and effect in this manner does not take into consideration the possibility of processes intervening between the *"A"* and the *"B,"* a more useful conception for the advanced sciences, such as physics, is to state a law in the form of a differential equation which indicates what is tending to occur. Since multiplicity of causes yielding one or more effects is the usual occurrence in nature, a law is written stating the relationship among many variables. Any of these physical laws can be disproved by experience, but none proved by it. Physical laws assert more than experience alone allows. We believe that an object exists when we do not see it, but cannot prove this by experience.

Meaning of Empirical Statements of Laws

How is any empirical statement of a law to be verified and/or interpreted as meaningful? To state that all future consequences of a general proposition are true is itself a proposition of which the specific instances cannot be enumerated. If I hold the hypothesis that the table exists only when I look at it, and another holds that the table exists when neither I nor any one else is looking at it, the testable consequences of both hypotheses are exactly the same. If meaning is to be identified with verification then these two hypotheses have the same meaning. Russell concludes that the two hypotheses should not have the same consequences and, hence, that seeking the meaning of a proposition in its consequences leads only to other propositions and so on, through an infinite regress. The difficulty lies in an insistence on experience for inference and verification. We must have reasons in advance of experience for believing that some given event will occur. The turning point of Russell's discussion is contained in his statement that inference of something not experienced is not inference of something nameable, but rather the truth of an existence proposition. If induction is valid, in whatever cases, it is possible to know existence propositions without knowing any particular instance of their truth. These inductive inferences, going beyond experience, always involve causation.

There is one among several kinds of causation listed by Russell which is of particular importance for our discussion in Chapter Five. Causation has been considered, up to this point, as a kind of line or succession of events, whereby one event in the future is expected because of the presence of another event and knowledge of the mode of connection of the events. However, it is also possible that an event may be affected by a series of antecedent and current events whereby a patterning of events mutually influencing each other occurs. The example given is that of the collision among billiard balls in the game of pool. There are various interconnected relationships between the speed and direction of the various balls. If a single ball had been moving in a slightly different direction or at a slightly different speed, the speed and direction of some or all of the other balls would have been changed. The action of any single ball can be predicted by a causal law of the kind discussed above, but when the ball collides with another, the causal law allows a much restricted inference concerning the single ball. Something besides induction along causal lines is needed, and this is observation of the interaction of the previously separable causal lines by which inference was possible for the movement of each ball separately. The observation of the interaction of the various balls can tell us about the various patterning of the movement of the balls only *after* it occurs. Induction to the future has no place in this process. For prediction to be possible, various causal lines will have to be disentangled and utilized as an integrated set. However, Russell points out that inference to unobserved occasions is possible. Thus, the motion of similar balls on a similar table at another time would probably follow the same field principles as those discovered from observing the balls on our table. This consideration of interaction as a special kind of causation is particularly important for an examination of the assumptions of the social psychological systems derived from Kant, continuing through Brentano, the gestalters, and eventually to Kurt Lewin who presents a "field" interpretation of social interaction. Later we shall see how the billiard balls may be replaced with people, and reasoning about their actions from observed relations to one another and to objects becomes possible.

While we have focused upon only two of them (2 and 3), Russell lists five postulates required to validate scientific method, and by implication cause and effect, as a legitimate inferential technique. They are:

1. The postulate of quasi-permanence.
2. The postulate of separable causal lines.
3. The postulate of spatio-temporal continuity in causal lines.
4. The postulate of the common causal origin of similar structures ranged about a center, or, more simply: the structural postulate.
5. The postulate of analogy.

These postulates are to be taken as *a priori,* with belief in them based upon "animal inference," which has been described earlier in the chapter. These *a priori* postulates are tenable if they lead to more and more precise formulations which fewer and fewer people doubt. This conclusion directly influenced R. B. Braithwaite, who is more specific than Russell about the nature of the scientific explanation derived from an *a priori* base.

In summarizing Russell's position, which is the position of this book as well, concerning those elements of cause and effect which constitute the necessary conditions for successful inference, we may begin by considering what empiricism asserts. The central idea of empiricism is that all synthetic knowledge (in Kant's sense) is based upon experience. Yet we have statements, such as, "There is an event which no one perceives," which are intelligible to us. We can comprehend a sentence whose subject matter lies outside of experience because it uses words which are variables (in a mathematical sense) and have meaning within our experience. The words I understand are understandable through my experience. However, the truth or falsehood of the statement is not apprehensible through an understanding of the words in the sentence. What is required is that we have some knowledge of universal propositions which will allow us to judge the truth or falsity of statements which are not just existence propositions involving statements of empirical probability. Universal propositions based on perception alone apply only to the period of time taken up by the perception, and cannot indicate what is occurring when we are not in the act of perceiving. Presumably, Russell's five postulates, or similar postulates, may provide the needed universal propositions. These postulates cannot be deduced from facts of experience, as has already been demonstrated. "Either, therefore, we know something independently of experience, or science is moonshine" (Russell, 1949, p. 505). Experience must be supplemented by causal principles which are known *a priori,* in order to infer unexamined, that is, future or unobserved cases. As Pap has stated, "The principle of causality, therefore, is not analytic, nor is it an inductive generalization that could be refuted by contrary instances.

It is best described as a *guiding principle* of causal inquiry that owes its successes to a contingent feature of the universe" (1962, p. 311).

R. B. Braithwaite

It is now possible to broaden our discussion of cause and effect to include techniques whereby science assigns meaning to its various concepts. To be sure, cause and effect still plays its part in the inferential process. It is the assignment of meaning, as discussed by modern philosophers of science, in conjunction with the historically prior ideas of causation already examined, that will provide the major base for our later analyses.

The assignment of meaning to statements which imply a cause and effect relationship between two or more events may best be understood within the context of theory construction in science, and especially in psychology. It is possible to illustrate this by examining the work of R. B. Braithwaite (1960) concerning the nature of scientific explanation.

Braithwaite is concerned with scientific laws and their public meaning, and is not concerned with the transition of private thought to the public domain. He concentrates upon showing that scientific statements depend only upon the constant conjunction view of causation. Admittedly, Hume's view of causation as constant conjunction of events is not adequate for handling the nature of modern scientific law. Braithwaite rejects the idea, maintained by many thinkers since Aristotle, that there is an "extra element," usually referring to logical necessity, contained in the cause and effect relationship. Therefore, Kant's position, by implication, is also rejected. Braithwaite admits that induction by simple enumeration is not sufficient to establish the generalizations of science. A generalization must be considered within the context of the scientific system of which it is a part. The method by which we establish hypotheses within a scientific system is therefore of central importance in discovering meaning within the system. An understanding of this method will also further clarify the nature of causality in its most modern use.

Braithwaite has set himself the task of showing how a position based upon Hume's idea of constant conjunction, with the addition of a doctrine concerning the use of generalizations within a scientific system, can essentially avoid the problem of involving logical and/or other *a priori* principles to explain the nature of meaning in science. Taking this position, he has already moved toward a point of view which cannot be completely Humean because he includes generalizations which are not based solely on constant conjunction. Braithwaite makes a point of great significance for current research strategies in psychology. He takes the position that the constant conjunction point of view regarding the nature of scientific empirical inference is the most conservative position one may take. If sufficient caution is exercised by a theorist, and only tentative generalizations based upon calculated probabilities are made in a given enumerative situation, these generalizations are more likely to hold than any others associated with the same data, *caeteris paribus*. Modern behaviorists, such as B. F. Skinner, have emphasized this point in other ways. However, taking this position, what one gains in precision may be lost with respect to relevance to important problems. This is especially true in psychology.

Since the process of induction has already been shown to be related to causality, it is perhaps useful to summarize Braithwaite's interpretation of it. He generally agrees with Russell, but describes the successful inductive inference as a process whereby an inductive conclusion is derived from empirical premises in accordance with one or more principles of inductive inference. These principles can be divided into two major types, simple enumeration and elimination. In the case of simple enumeration, an inductive hypothesis is taken to be well established if it has not been refuted by experience and has been confirmed by a number of positive instances, in accordance with some minimum expectation established as a policy for that induction. The principle of elimination holds that an inductive hypothesis is taken to be well established if it has not been refuted by experience and if alternative hypotheses have been refuted by experience. The justification of induction lies in the principle of inductive inference that is used in the induction. There are rules of procedure for making inductive inferences, either by simple enumeration or by elimination, which can be found in any book on logic and the scientific method. The justification of induction as a valid principle depends upon the justification of these rules of procedure. Inductive procedure is used by scientists because of its predictive value. It yields hypotheses from which testable consequences can be deduced that are found to be true. The validity of this process depends upon the establishment of the reasonableness of following such a procedure, and on an argument to refute the charge of circularity which is usually made against this type of defense of the validity of induction. The charge of circularity is formulated in the following manner: The validity of every inductive inference presupposes the validity of induction by simple enumeration, and the validity of induction by simple enumeration presupposes its own validity. Although Braithwaite argues extensively in attempting to deny circularity in the inductive procedure, his main contention is that there is no error in utilizing the effectiveness of a policy of inference to justify an inference to this effectiveness. The justification of any inference, inductive or deductive, begins with a reasonable belief in the initial steps of the inferential process. We must reasonably believe, for example, that the syllogism is a meaningful way to proceed in reaching certain true conclusions. There is no external justification for belief in the validity of this aspect of deductive logic.

Braithwaite's argument has the character of an attempt to justify an individual's personal belief; that is, the subjective process of passing from a mere belief in a conclusion to a reasonable belief through the use of an inductive inference. Since this is the case, he argues, justification is not circular because making a successful inference has itself added an increment of belief to the individual. His argument is as follows: The conditions for it to be subjectively valid for a man to infer *e,* the proposition that induction by simple enumeration is effective, from enumerative evidence for *e,* and, correlatively, that this belief, obtained or supportable by this inference, is a subjectively reasonable belief are, first, that he should reasonably believe the evidence for *e,* and secondly, that he should believe *e.* Since neither of these conditions includes the requirement that his belief in *e* should be a reasonable one, there is no explicit circularity in his reasoning. Nor is there any implicit circularity, since he can quite well reasonably believe both that he is reasonable in believing the enumerative evidence for *e,* and that he is believing *e,* without reasonably believing, or indeed believing at all, that he is reasonable in thus believing *e.* Braithwaite further states that "the account of objective validity of an inference which has been given is in terms of the right working of an inference-machine, and . . . the implicit circularity only arises from the inference-machine becoming self-conscious about the way in which it operates" (1960, p. 291). The linkage between the objective validity and the subjective validity of induction is the effectiveness of the belief in the validity. Effectiveness is, in turn, established by a confirmation of an expectation held by the inferrer. The fact that Braithwaite makes the analogy of conceiving man to be an inference-making machine with "right working" principles indicates an almost Kantian belief in internal principles which are necessary for understanding certain aspects of subjective (phenomenal) reality. The constant conjunction view, as proposed by Hume, is used as a method of connecting this phenomenal experience with the presumably objective, external world. That is, one's inference is effective when his expectations are fulfilled with regard to some aspect of the external world. Incidentally, a tacit assumption is made that a world of empirical objects exists which is external to the understanding individual.

Braithwaite accepts Hume's notion of causality as constant conjunction, and bases his acceptance on his own argument for the validity of induction. However, this argument depends heavily upon the nature of the belief system of the individual making the induction as described above. Since Braithwaite does not explain the belief system of the individual making the induction by reference to experience, it follows that his view of causality as constant conjunction presupposes an individual whose inductive behavior is controlled by his characteristics as an "inference-making machine." Braithwaite makes a clear distinction between the deductive and inductive processes of a scientific system, assigning the idea of necessity as found in causality to the inductive process. It is not clear, however, whether this process of induction is free from the kinds of assumptions Russell makes in his analysis.

Cause and effect enter into Braithwaite's system as a statement of natural law, roughly synonymous with Russell's causal law, and with the idea of two or more events linked because of some necessary connection between them. For Braithwaite, any law-like statement gains validity from one or both of two sources: The statement's instances are validated either by induction, or by their holding a logically necessary position within the context of a series of hypothetico-deductive statements. The extra ingredient in a cause and effect type of statement, besides constant conjunction of relevant events (which can be validated by induction), is its logical position within an entire hypothetico-deductive system. This position constitutes the logical necessity of any given cause and effect statement. With this discovery, Braithwaite believed he simply extended Hume's constant conjunction view. In reality, he has combined Hume's position with recognition of a man-created logical system which supplies the ingredient of necessity. Any derivable empirical consequence of a hypothetico-deductive system can and must be validated by recourse to induction by simple enumeration of one of its variants. However, unless the nature of the rules of logical deduction are in turn made amenable to inductive verification, it cannot account for the total meaning of a causal statement. Since any generalization within an established deductive system appears as a deduction from higher-level hypotheses which have been established independently of the generalization, it cannot be validated by the evidence validating the higher-level hypotheses. These principles of connection must be established by different evidence, or by other principles. As Russell and others have pointed out, one would be hard pressed to show that the validation of these principles is based on induction. Hence, we are turned back again to some form of validation by *a priori* principles.

Conclusions

Braithwaite sees necessary connection as a tendency to think of volitional action as most relevant to an everyday use of the idea of cause and effect. To want to do something is associated with cause, and the something done, with effect. The apparent connection of the cause and the effect is part of the individual's process of volitional intent. According to Braithwaite, *science does not use the concept in this manner*. One feels that Braithwaite believes he has laid to rest necessary connection in the cause and effect sequence. Braithwaite meaningfully locates the context into which necessary connections must be placed, that is, in the deductive scheme in which any single statement of constant conjunction is found. However, no sequence or pairing of events through constant conjunction alone is sufficient to contain all of the meaning we intend in making a causal statement. The extra element of necessary connection must be present, Braithwaite to the contrary notwithstanding. He has provided an interpretation of necessary connection by emphasizing the deductive system from which our statement of constant conjunction of specific events is derivable. The problem now is whether or not a causal statement, based upon constant conjunction of events, can legitimately be causal if it is not contained within a deductive system. Certainly, one can make a statement of constant conjunction between two classes of events which has no position within a deductive system. It would be difficult to imagine the statement having any law-like properties, however, if it were not so contained. We might note that the number of mules and the number of professors in several states were inversely correlated, but the fullest meaning of this observation would be found in an analysis of the states' agricultural, educational, and socio-political structures. Our original statement of constant conjunction would be "explained" when placed within a system of explanation of which it was a derivative expectation. As Braithwaite notes, "the nature of scientific laws cannot be treated independently of their function within a deductive system" (1960, p. 339).

In the concluding paragraphs of his excellent book, Braithwaite reiterates his opposition to a Kantian epistemology and tacitly renews his support of a Humean approach:

> To what extent, then, should an established scientific deductive system be regarded as a free creation of the human mind, and to what extent should it be regarded as giving an objective account of the facts of nature?
>
> This question would be difficult and important if we wished to maintain, with Kant, that some of the features of scientific laws were products of the human mind, so that in knowing such a law we were reading in nature something which we had written in the mental act of knowing. It would then be essential for a philosopher of science to distinguish between what was to be put down to Nature and what to the knowing mind in each scientific law. If we do not take the Kantian standpoint, the question becomes merely that of distinguishing between what is due to Nature and what is due to our powers of representing by means of our statements and formulae an ordered system of scientific laws, the answer to which is easy to give. Nature does not provide separately both facts and laws; our statements of laws are a way of describing observed facts and of predicting facts at present unobserved. *The form of a statement of a scientific hypothesis, and its use to express a general proposition, is a human device;* what is due to Nature are the observable facts which refute or fail to refute the scientific hypothesis. The meaning of all the symbols we use—those we use for denoting features of our immediate experience as well as the theoretical terms which we use with a sophisticated interpretation—*is determined by our decision to use them in the way we do* (1960, p. 367, italics Lana's).

Braithwaite seems not to realize that the human device of forming scientific or other statements intending general propositions, and our use of terms in a theoretical system, are the very features of the epistemological process upon which Kant focussed. These processes cannot be divorced from the total scientific enterprise of developing theoretical systems of explanation. Although many different approaches to scientific knowledge are possible, they all possess elements which are similar and which provide part of the meaning base for the total effort. The ideas associated with causality, as discussed throughout this chapter, seem to be of this nature.

chapter

3

Other Philosophical Problems

The resolution regarding a useful, and perhaps correct, interpretation of cause and effect must be put aside until later chapters. In the present chapter, we shall pursue further the implications of the epistemologies of Hume and Kant, selecting a number of individuals to indicate the line of influence to modern thinking in social psychology.

Hume's formulation of cause and effect had an enormous impact on science, which was considered a fundamentally anti-metaphysical discipline. Hume's belief that functional relationships among variables supplied the basic bit of information provided an apologia for the kinds of conclusions scientists found themselves most comfortable in drawing anyway. Perhaps because greater agreement was possible when sense data instead of abstract assumptions were used as the basis of conclusion drawing, science became extremely conservative in making conclusions, and sought the narrower, certain principle rather than the broader, tenuous one. After all, conclusions based on a set of functional contingencies among observed variables entail less error than those based on the fact that a set of conditions necessarily follows, as a product, from the prior appearance of another set of conditions. Mach, at least by implication, had this well incorporated into his thinking. Concern with necessity in the causal inferential situation is absent from, or at least very much de-emphasized in, Mach's (1959) work, *Analysis of Sensations,* to which we now turn.

Mach infused into a philosophy of science, that is, into a method of procedure, Hume's fundamental observation. He bridges the gap between Humean causality and the largely implicit assumptive base of behaviorism, best represented by B. F. Skinner. For our purposes, the important aspects of Mach's thinking center around his attempt to show that the concept of ego is superfluous in an explanation of human behavior, and around his analysis of the nature of the process of sensation.

Mach discusses ideas such as the "thing-in-itself" and the ego as summary devices for collections of elements. Used first as a short-hand by the individual, the summary device eventually becomes an entity in itself in the process of conceptualization. Let us take a given, "permanent," perceptual complex for an example. Were we to re-move a small part, we would still see the permanent complex and call it by the same name. We can take away any given part without destroying the complex. Hence, we might imagine that the complex has a quality, the "thing-in-itself," which remains when all parts are removed. We have confused the label, first used as a convenience to denote a totality of elements, with a presumed property called "essence" or the "thing-in-itself." Mach concludes that objects are composed of various elements in various combinations, and that an object is fully comprehended when we understand what its com-ponent elements are, and their manner of connection.

The concept "ego" falls under this analysis, for it is a summary device, denoting a set of characteristics, and without an existence of its own. Once recognized as a summary device, useful only for prac-tical purposes, the ego disappears as a concept. A series of elements remain, their various connections discernible through careful exami-nation. There is no separation between the ego and the rest of the world, for there can be no true dichotomy between physical and mental. All dualisms are therefore rejected. A monism recognizing no essential differences between sensation (appearance) and thing replaces the usual dualism which separates sensation from its physical object. It is only in the functional dependence between an object and an observer that the term "sensation" is meaningful.

Thus, perceptions, presentations, volitions, and emotions, in short the whole inner and outer world, are put together, in combinations of varying evanescence and permanence, out of a small number of homogeneous elements. The aim of *all research* is to ascertain the mode of connexion of these elements. . . . For us colors, sounds, spaces, times . . . are provisionally the ultimate elements whose given connexion it is our business to investigate (Mach, 1959, pp. 22, 29-30, italics Lana's).

The colors, sounds, etc., are inherent neither in the physical objects involved, nor in the characteristics of the perceiver, but are products of the interaction of the two, rendering dualism unnecessary. Mach's methodology seeks the functional relations among experiences. Any reference to a thing-in-itself, or to any other "fundamental variable," becomes superfluous.

For Mach, complexes of colors, sounds and other sensations, usually called bodies, are denoted by the letters A, B, C. . . . The complex of colors, sounds, etc., which is part of the former complex $(A, B, C . . .)$, but which can be distinguished from it by certain peculiarities, is denoted by K, L, M. . . . The complex composed of memory-images, volitions, feelings and others is represented by α, β, γ. . . . In common but incorrect thinking, the complexes $\alpha, \beta, \gamma . . . K, L, M . . .$, taken together, are conceived as the ego. The ego is thought to contrast with bodies $(A, B, C . . .)$ existing external to the other two sets of complexes. At first glance $A, B, C . . .$ appears to be independent of the ego and opposed to it with a separate existence. However, many changes in $\alpha, \beta, \gamma . . .$ do pass by way of changes in $K, L, M . . .$ to $A, B, C . . .$, and vice versa. Mach gives an example of

when powerful ideas burst forth into acts, or when our environment induces noticeable changes in our body. At the same time the group $K, L, M . . .$ appears to be more intimately connected with $\alpha, \beta, \gamma . . .$ and with $A, B, C . . .$ than the latter with one another; and their relations find their expression in common thought and speech (1959, p. 9).

The group *A, B, C* . . . always is determined in part by *K, L, M.* . . . The physical characteristics of an object depend upon the conditions within the organism, and upon the relations between object and organism (e.g., distance, light available), at a given time. In short, the nature of perception makes the idea of the separation of object and organism, of object and ego, extremely difficult to maintain. "The properties of one and the same body, therefore, appear modified by our own body; they appear conditioned by it. But where, now, is that *same* body, which appears so *different?* All that can be said is, that with different *K, L, M* . . . different *A, B, C* . . . are associated" (Mach, 1959, pp. 9, 10).

The fundamental data of science, for physicists as well as for psychologists, are sensations. They are not analyzable into either physical entities or psychological entities, but are products of both kinds of data. There need be no difficulty for the physicist or for the psychologist in understanding each other's data. Here, then, is the unity of science conceived on the basis of an empiricist idea of the priority of sensation in all epistemology. Mach assumes that physical objects external to oneself exist without further demonstration; given his orientation, this is, of course, the only way he can handle the problem of objects outside of sensation. From this it also follows that differences traditionally conceived to exist between sensation and perception do not actually exist.

Like Hume, Mach emphasizes that contiguity of events is central to the causal process. We see the close relationship between both philosophers and modern American psychology in this epistemological aspect. Rejecting the traditional conception of cause, as discussed in Chapter One, Mach suggests it be replaced by the mathematical concept of function; that is, by the "dependence of the characteristics of phenomena on one another" (Mach, 1959, p. 89). The goal of research is not simply a mathematical sum of sensations, but the development of mathematical functions. These relationships among sensations might range from linear to complex curvilinear.

In Mach's book, little reference is made to theory and its nature, in contrast to Professor Braithwaite's book, which turns upon such a discussion. Mach is one of the earliest and best known scientific a-theorists:

> I should like the scientists to realize that my view eliminates all metaphysical questions indifferently, whether they be only regarded as insoluble at the present moment, or whether they be regarded as meaningless for all time. I should like them, further, to reflect that everything that we can know about the world is necessarily expressed in the sensations, which can be set free from the individual influence of the observer in a precisely definable manner. Everything that we can want to know is given by the solution of a problem in mathematical form, by the ascertainment of the functional dependence of the sensational elements on one another. This knowledge exhausts the knowledge of "reality." The bridge between physics, in the widest sense, and scientific psychology, is formed of these very elements, which are physical and psychical objects according to the kind of combination that is being investigated (Mach, 1959, p. 369).

The Ego Concept

We have established that Mach believed that the ego is a provisional idea, used for initial orientation, which should disappear on analysis of the relevant bodily, physical, and psychological elements. This assumption discounts the possibility that, since all individuals believe in, or act as if they possessed a separate ego (a point with which Mach would agree), there may be a degree of scientific validity in examining this concept. Mach makes a reductive jump and states that comprehension of individual behavior or action is based on functional relationships of the individual's elements composed of central processes, physical environmental stimuli, and aspects of his own body. If the ego is not just a summary label, however, but a unique human process or processes, then Mach can never fully understand the nature of human beings. What are called the "higher processes" in man, such as memory, reasoning, thinking, and creativity, may be processes that are ordinarily conceived of as ego processes, and may not be reducible to Mach's elements. The class of elements which Mach identifies as volitions, memories, images, etc., may be what other theorists call ego processes. Furthermore, the validity of Mach's reduction remains a problem. The research or observations performed by Mach or his followers would be very different from that performed by those who conceive of the ego as non-reducible. Mach, like Hume, recognized that man acts as if he has an ego (or for Hume, man acts as if there is such a thing as productive cause) and, like Hume, assumed man to be acting incorrectly. Mach removed an ancient prejudice from the scientific study of man, but he replaced it with a subtle one of his own: the compulsory reduction of complex or summary concepts to simpler ones. But there is no doubt that Mach cleared away many useless and archaic methodologies and concepts, particularly in psychology.

Mach's conclusion that the fundamental datum of science for both physicists and psychologists is sensation strongly influenced later phenomenalism, especially gestalt. Gestalt psychologists were to assume the fundamental unity of scientific explanation, making sensation (perception) the central datum in their investigations. Mach's statement that colors, sounds, etc., are inherent only as the product of the interaction of the physical objects and the characteristics of the perceiver, allowed the gestalt psychologists to emphasize the examination of the total configuration of object and perceiver. It also contributed to the gestalt formulation of isomorphism between behavioral (in the gestalt sense) processes and physiological processes. Mach called this concept *"the principle of the complete parallelism of the psychical and physical"* (1959, p. 60).

Since Mach so greatly influenced the central ideas in the systems of behaviorism and gestalt psychology, his influence on social psychological theorizing is only one step removed from theirs.

The Data of Science

We have discussed so far two interpretations of cause and effect, the one functional, the other, in some manner, productive. However, we have not distinguished the nature of an empirical study in applying one or both interpretations. When one regards the subject matter of physics, chemistry, or biology, for example, the observational and inferential processes of the scientist never directly enter, as data, the theoretical or observed subject matter of the given discipline. One position (Mach, 1959) is that the observational and inferential processes of all science are the same. That is, the perceptions of the scientist are subject to the same laws whether he be psychologist or physicist. Furthermore, although the scientist brings concepts and techniques which are partly determined by his specific discipline, he does not intend to study them. (I am referring to the conceptual determination of factual observation, and not to interference effects of observation, common both to microphysics and psychology [see Lana, 1968].)

Yet in psychology, sociology, and anthropology, the subject matter is often indistinguishable from the scientist's observational and inferential processes. This may make a difference in the kinds of inferences made by social scientists. If one follows Hume, Mach, and the behaviorist tradition, it is allowable that the scientist dealing with human activity proceeds in essentially the same way as a physical scientist dealing with the data of his discipline. That is, one may observe human behavior, record it, and theorize about it, in the same manner as a physicist would when observing the movement of a planet. Much human activity, such as that involved in the conditioning of a simple response, is of this nature. So much has been written describing the theorizing of behavioristically oriented psychologists, and its similarity to theorizing in physics, that we need not discuss it here. On the other hand, when the subject matter is one of man's higher processes, such as problem solving, reasoning, or creative thought, the scientist's approach may itself be part of the process he is studying. It would seem that his theorizing must be concerned with the discipline's own conceptual tools. This position is in the tradition of Kant and German idealism and of modern gestalt psychology. It would not be quite correct to say, however, that different theoretical positions regarding human activity such as behaviorism and gestalt psychology can be principally characterized by this difference. Nor is it completely evident that within each general theoretical orientation specific theories follow one assumption or the other.

At this point, we see that there are two distinct theoretical approaches to the study of human activity: the functional, and the holistic. The argument for the validity of either of these approaches usually begins with support of, or opposition to, the idea that any segment of social behavior can be reduced, without loss of meaning, to the concepts and terms of individual psychology. Theorists working within a functional approach usually accept the possibility of further reduction of the terms of social activity, rather than show that such terms have already been reduced. If such a reduction is possible both logically and empirically, then a functional analysis of social behavior is preferable to the holistic analysis. If it were not, the holistic analysis would be preferable. Certainly, such a demonstration might well change the way the researcher performed his research. It would also undoubtedly alter his theoretical concepts and his conclusions. It will be fruitful to examine the possibility of the non-reducibility of social activity from a logical point of view, before proceeding to specific theories.

Our conception of what belongs to the world, that is, of what "reality" consists, is given to us largely by our language. Some psychologists interpret the acquisition and use of language as an almost totally learned phenomenon. Functional interpretations of the acquisition and use of language have been attempted although most are not convincing in their premise that the acquisition and use of language is best explained by the reduction of conceptual elements to simpler, non-conceptual entities (e.g., Chomsky, 1959; Miller, 1965). There has been an underestimation of the role of the *a priori* in concept analysis, as there had been an overestimation of it by earlier thinkers. Understanding what constitutes social behavior such as the use of language may be principally a problem in conceptual analysis, rather than one of isolating relevant functional contingencies. Actually, the two problems dove-tail. Social relations, language, and expressions of reality all involve normative behavior by individuals who accept and understand the rules involved. In short, correct language usage and social behavior are discovered only through contact with other people who reinforce the rules which they understand and accept as well.

It may be that many concepts are not formed through the process of generalization, invoked in the usual functional explanation. The possession of *a priori* concepts (although not necessarily in the Kantian intuitive sense, but perhaps more in the manner described by Russell) is a necessary condition for obtaining generalizations. A process of generalizing probably does occur in animals and men, but it may be misleading to call the resulting product a "concept." We have indicated the difficulty in arguing that certain concepts such as cause and effect are the result of a process of empirical generalization. The concept already must be present for the inference to take place. It seems reasonably clear that the process of drawing an inference cannot be represented by a formula of any kind. It is in the context of human social activity that concepts, inferences and language in general derive any sense at all. An example given by Winch is well taken.

Suppose that *N,* a university lecturer, says that he is going to cancel his next week's lectures because he intends to travel to London: here we have a statement of intention for which a reason is given. Now *N* does not *infer* his intention of cancelling his lectures from his desire to go to London, as the imminent shattering of the glass might be inferred, either from the fact that someone had thrown a stone or from the brittleness of the glass. *N* does not offer his reason as *evidence* for the soundness of his prediction about his future behavior. Rather, he is *justifying* his intention. His statement is not of the form: "Such and such causal factors are present, therefore this will result"; nor yet of the form: "I have such and such a disposition, which will result in my doing this"; it is of the form: "In view of such and such considerations this will be a reasonable thing to do" (1958, p. 81).

The functionalist criticism is that even though Professor *N* reasons to himself in such a manner, he may be a relatively passive organism to various environmental and physiological contingencies, resulting not only in his actual behavior, but in his verbal explanation of why he behaves the way he does. The problem of how normative or, in Winch's terms, "rule following" behavior works, is not completely solved with Winch's analysis. Although Professor *N* may not observe a causal sequence in coming to his decision, an examination of his past life might lead one to predict the exact course of events which occurred and, also, *N*'s articulated reasons for doing what he did. A reductive analysis might have indicated a simpler more accurate set of contingencies allowing for greater prediction of his behavior, verbal and otherwise. There may be no way of telling whether rule following behavior limits our understanding of other human activity and, therefore, of our own behavior. What is clear is that if an individual infers anything at all he is limited by the nature of what it means to infer for human beings. But this does not mean, as Winch seems to suggest, that understanding social behavior always will be limited by the fact that the social scientist must operate under the conceptual system of the individuals he is studying. A reductive explanation might be discovered which would explain some or all aspects of social behavior, and without having the limits of the subject matter under examination. This, of course, implies an infinite regress in explanation, but then science has always proceeded on this basis quite successfully. The conclusion that an infinite regress in explanation is inevitable in any search for the reductive argument is no case against its pursuit. Let us re-examine Winch's example. Professor *N* might really have argued as follows: "If I intend to go to London next week, and I must assuredly do so, then I absolutely must cancel my lectures. That is, it is physically impossible for me to be in two places at the same time and, although I would like to attend my lecture, my London trip takes precedence. I therefore do *infer* (i.e., it follows causally) that I cannot be at my lecture next week and in London at the same time." The point is that the impossibility of being in two places at once is implied by Professor *N*'s statement of intention. I do not wish to deny that Professor *N* might have reasoned as Winch suggests, but he also might have reasoned as I suggested or the implied causal analysis might have been contained as part of the meaning of his statement of intentionality as given by Winch. A reductive analysis is possible. Yet, although the activity of scientists is governed by rules, as is the individual within a social context, it may be possible to discover through functional and/or physiological analysis reasons for the rules which are independent of their operation. However, the examination of social behavior is much more difficult than the study of other phenomena, not only because the subject matter is complex, but because the behavior of the scientist studying it is part of that subject matter.

In contrast, certain forms of social behavior are predictable for the very reason that they are not directly part of conceptual language structure. They may be studied in part without reference to the conceptual analysis which Winch and other theorists insist upon. In the area of opinion and attitude change, for example, factors which are non-conceptual may be crucial in determining change. These factors, such as the prestige of the communicator (Hovland, Janis and Kelley, 1953); the order of presentation of opposed communications (Hovland, 1957; Lana, 1961, 1963a,b,c, 1964a,b,c, 1966); and the style in which the communication is presented (Molnar, 1955); have been shown to affect the amount of opinion change after listening to persuasive communications. The most important aspects of social activity, however, may be found in the conceptual structure of language and, hence, the usual kinds of predictive systems of the natural sciences may be totally irrelevant to the understanding and prediction of such activity. We shall deal specifically with both conceptual and functional data and explanations utilized by various social psychologists as we examine specific systems in the following chapters. It remains only to be emphasized at this juncture that, although social activity and man's inferential processes may be indistinguishable from one another, there may also be a logically conceivable, more reduced level of explanation that predicts or explains one or both phenomena.

Our task in the chapter has been to indicate the dichotomy in thinking about social behavior. Is social behavior principally a conceptual *a priori* or is it reducible to a series of simpler functional contingencies which are parts of what we conceive to be social activity? We cannot champion one view at the expense of the other because both are essentially correct. However, we can examine specific theories for validity keeping our discussion up to this point in mind.

part
II

The Systems

Having established some of the crucial assumptions regarding causality and reduction, we now turn to the major systems in contemporary social psychology. We have grouped them in the following way: "Functional-Reductive Theories" (Chapter Four), "Holistic Theories" (Chapter Five), "Psychoanalysis and the Instinctive Basis of Social Activity" (Chapter Six), and "The Theory of Cognitive Dissonance" (Chapter Seven). The functional-reductive theories, partially derived from Hume, possess the characteristics of the contingency interpretation of cause and effect as well as the possibility for an eventual reduction of terms. Bandura and Walters' system is included in Chapter Four because it represents a theory which is functional in approach without being reductive. It provides an example of how a theory might avoid a reductive bias without yielding its functional emphasis. The holistic theories, more consistent with the Kantian position on cause and effect than are the functional-reductive theories, lend themselves to an anti-reductionist framework. However, we shall see that the matter is not quite so simple as I have expressed it here. Psychoanalytic theories and the theory of cognitive dissonance are discussed separately since their implicit stance with respect to the nature of causality and reduction does not fit easily under the functional-reductive or holistic theories.

To analyze the assumptions of the various theories, it will be necessary to modify our approach and give expositions of the various theories to clarify the relevant principles. We shall be dealing with specific empirically-based theories, and will discuss the possibilities and limitations of each. We shall see a sharpening of the Hume-Kant split which was beginning to be articulated by Mach, although none was apparent to either of those philosophers when they wrote their principal works. Some general attention will be paid to methodology, for it is impossible to separate it from theory in an empirically-based system.

chapter

4

The Functional-Reductive
Theories

The basic terms of the theories in this chapter are tentative.
These terms are possibly the macro-terms of a more inclusive system
which will eventually be formulated. Social psychological theories of
the functional-reductive type usually include terms appropriate to
individual psychology, and many theorists of this persuasion believe
that these terms eventually will be reduced to terms ordinarily found
in physiology. It is also characteristic of these theories that their
principles or postulates or hypotheses were originally developed as
generalizations from observations of functional contingencies of empirical events.

I am excluding theories dependent on formal postulates from
which empirical generalizations are derived, such as Clark Hull's
(1943), which have been used to explain aspects of social behavior,
such as social drive (e.g., Dollard and Miller, 1954), and security
behavior in human beings. The degree of success of this type of explanation is problematic, however. Although functional-reductive approaches abound in American psychology, especially within the tradition of behaviorism, few such systems deal with the totality of human
social activity. This is not accidental, however, and we shall be concerned with the reasons for this below.

B. F. Skinner

The first and foremost functional-reductive theory of social activity is rarely thought of as a theory of social activity at all. B. F. Skinner (1953) himself has pointed out that he had not developed a theory of behavior but, rather, a technique for gathering empirical contingencies among various events which then could be used to predict behavior. Whatever the degree of formality of Skinner's theoretical thinking, he does make certain implicit assumptions which greatly affect the kinds of results it is possible for him to obtain.

Of the contemporary psychological systems derived from Hume and the English empiricist tradition, Skinner's is the most consistent with that tradition and adds the fewest assumptions. Skinner's uncomplex epistemology is practically identical to Hume's. He is compelling because of his genius in behavioral engineering and in his ability to discover the environmental-organismic contingencies which at one time were considered too complex to be analyzed into simple behavioral components. To date Skinner has made the best empirical, scientific translation of Hume and Mach,[1] although it seems unlikely that this was his intention.

There are three important assumptions in Skinner's approach. The first is that human activity, that is, "behavior," is determined by variables which are potentially discoverable. There is no such thing as spontaneous human activity, with the possible exception of non-directed bodily movements such as are found in infants. And even these are traceable to physiological conditions functioning within the organism. Skinner's assumption is common to the other disciplines of science, and to most psychologists who nevertheless take varying theoretical positions with respect to the nature of human behavior.

[1] As we have seen in Chapter Three, both modern behaviorism and gestalt psychology have been given impetus by Ernst Mach. Besides his insistence on analysis and reduction of all theoretical concepts, Mach emphasized the need to focus upon a totally functioning organism in explaining human activity.

The second assumption represents the core of his approach, and we need to follow it in some of its ramifications. To Skinner, the most parsimonious and fruitful approach to the discovery of generalizations about the nature of human activity is a functional one, consisting of relationships between independent environmental variables and dependent response variables of the organism's behavioral repertoire. Contingencies among the variables constitute the functional predictive generalizations of behavior. This approach minimizes errors of generalization and those associated with the over-abundant use of theoretical entities (e.g., ego, drive, habit, etc.). Cause and effect are identified only with independent and dependent variables respectively, in the manner of Hume. A sub-assumption is that the immediate environment and the environmental history of the organism are the major sources of independent (input, causal) variables affecting dependent (output, effect) variables.

Another sub-assumption is that all human behavior may be examined in this functional input-output manner, and that this is the best way to understand human activity. It seems probable that Skinner would claim that his system is not categorically the best approach to these problems, but that it has been successful to some degree already and should be given an opportunity to be applied to some of the more complex problems of human behavior. We shall consider that the universal applicability of the system has been implied by Skinner, using his novel, *Walden II,* as support.

The third assumption is that functional relations are reducible to physiological entities which must be directly observable and not hypothetical. Reduction of these physiological entities to biochemical and eventually physical terms is not possible at present, but it is probable that it will be at some future time. The functional approach necessarily allows for the possibility of change in its referents to those of a higher (more reduced) status. Actually this third assumption follows from the second and may not technically be a separate assumption but rather a derivative corollary to it. However, to make it as clear as possible we articulate it as such here.

Two of Skinner's terms must be defined. An "operant" is any class of responses about which we are interested in making predictions. It is the predictive unit of Skinner's behavior system. "Reinforcement," or, more precisely, "operant reinforcement," refers to the situation where the appearance of a reinforcer (reward or punishment) is contingent upon a response being made by the organism. The response of "raising the head" is an operant; giving food to an animal immediately after he has raised his head is operant reinforcement.

We need next to examine the implications of such a system for understanding human social activity. As have others before him, Skinner (1957) recognized that the formation and nature of verbal behavior were of central importance in understanding interaction among human beings. Verbal behavior constitutes in humans both the principal means of communication and the basis for abstract and creative thinking. This is accepted by theorists of all persuasions. A fundamental aspect of verbal behavior for Skinner is that in its formation and use by the human organism it is subject to the same principles of behavior as any non-verbal operant. Reinforcement is the mechanism of connection between a verbal response and its preceding independent stimulus variables, as it is in the case of a non-verbal operant. The relevant external variables can be the rewards that a mother offers a child for performing a desired activity. Candy, stroking, or affection offered after a child has made a verbal response increases the probability that the response will reappear under similar stimulus circumstances. If we consider the learning of nouns by a child, the process would be one of inducing the verbal response by pronouncing it in the presence of the child and rewarding (reinforcing) the child with the object represented by the correct response word; for example, candy would be given to the child upon his pronouncing the word "candy." The learning and subsequent use of verbs, adjectives, phrases, and whole sentences are explained in a like manner; the operants become more complex, but their appearance is still under the influence of an identifiable reinforcement. The success of Skinner's treatment would depend upon the predictability of the desired verbal response, given previous knowledge of the operants and their degrees of reinforcement in the history of the organism. Admittedly, the problem of prediction is more complex than in a situation where a non-verbal form of response constitutes the dependent variable. When Skinner considers how the individual's verbal responses are acquired, his analysis departs from the usual semantic-syntactical focus.

We are concerned with Skinner's analysis of language in its complex forms, such as thinking, logic, scientific usage, and creativity, since these forms of expression relate to the adult social context. Skinner's classification of verbal behavior consists of dividing a repertoire of responses into various classes such as the mand, tact, echoic response, textual and interverbal behavior. In all of these, the response is controlled by various aspects of the environment or by the past history of the organism. A situation where the speaker himself seems to be the director and organizer of verbal behavior produces responses such as "if," "that," "before," "I guess," "I estimate," "I believe," "I concede," "I infer." This class of responses is called "autoclitic." Skinner argues that autoclitics, in which the attendant reinforcement contingencies are not as obvious as in other forms of verbal responses, are derivative from the other forms of verbal behavior which are subject to such reinforcement. Grammar and syntax are considered to be autoclitic processes. This form of verbal response, in which the individual speaker seems to be in control, is most often found in the processes of thinking, logic, and creativity. His analysis is quite similar to that of Hume and Kant. Notice that Skinner considered such a verbal response as "I infer" to be an autoclitic response derived from simpler forms of reinforced operants.

Skinner states that

There are at least two systems of responses, one based upon the other. The upper level can only be understood in terms of its relation to the lower. The notion of an inner self is an effort to represent the fact that when behavior is compounded in this way, the upper system seems to guide or alter the lower. But the controlling system is itself also behavior. The speaker may "know what he is saying" in the sense in which he "knows" any part or feature of the environment. Some of his behavior (the "known") serves as a variable in control of other parts ("knowing"). Such "propositional attitudes" as assertion, negation, and quantification, the design achieved through reviewing and rejecting or emitting responses, the generation of quantities of verbal behavior merely as such, and the highly complex manipulations of verbal thinking can all, as we shall see, be analyzed in terms of behavior which is evoked by or acts upon other behavior of the speaker. (1957, p. 313)

Man may listen to what he has spoken, or read what he has written, and make statements about these responses the way he would have had they been made by someone else. In so doing the autoclitic is born; presumably it is also explained. Skinner's analysis extends to various types of autoclitics but the kind of explanation remains the same. The reader is encouraged to check the exact arguments in Skinner's book.

If we examine the acquisition and use of the autoclitic "I infer," we see that it consists of the description of a relation between the autoclitic and other verbal behavior of the individual. When someone says "I infer," he recognizes that the observation that follows these words has previously occurred after some earlier verbal response. For example, one might say, "In the past, when I have observed myself responding to a given stimulus configuration with the words, 'this is made of chocolate,' I have afterwards found myself responding with the words, 'I like it.' Therefore, in the future, when I am confronted with a chocolate dessert I have never eaten I say, '*I infer* that I will like it.' " Of course, these verbal responses would need to have been preceded in one's past history by the appropriate non-verbal behavior involving reinforcements with chocolate. This kind of analysis, often found to be inadequate by logicians and semanticists, is quite often the type which Skinner insists upon. Although I do not know whether or not he would approve of the above description, Skinner would readily admit that the phrase "I infer" is not necessarily a conscious verbalization proceeding as indicated above; but rather, that the history of this and many other kinds of verbal behavior developed in that manner earlier in the life of the individual. (See especially Chapters Fifteen and Sixteen in *Science and Human Behavior*.)

Thinking, then, is essentially a man talking to himself and utilizing a verbal repertoire provided by the social group, that is, the verbal community of which the individual is a part. Thought is be-havior and is not responsible for it. Hence, what is called the human mind is mostly, if not totally, amenable to study through behavioral analysis. However, Skinner recognizes that all human behavior, ver-bal or otherwise, "is subject to Kantian *a priori*'s in the sense that man as a behaving system has inescapable characteristics and limita-tions" (1957, p. 451). A good deal of the problem of the nature of human social behavior may turn on this admission. Actually, one may be rather surprised to read such a statement from a theorist who is considered a strict behaviorist. It is to Skinner's credit that he recognizes the possibility of certain characteristics in man's reactive system which affect certain response possibilities. However, the statement is concerned more with the limitations of human activity than with its characteristics. It may be that the Kantian categories, for example, represent not only the limitations and peculiar, but relatively unimportant, characteristics of man as a thinking, social organism, but also a part of his most essential characteristics. It may be that what is very important in understanding the nature of a think-ing, social being lies in an understanding of the nature of these *a priori* qualities. If this is the case, then by his own admission Skinner's behavioral operants may be totally irrelevant in explaining some aspects of thinking and many aspects of social activity. We shall discuss this problem in more detail in Chapter Nine after an examina-tion of the assumptions of other major theoretical approaches to social psychology. To the degree that thought is individual and non-communicative at the time it occurs, the truth about the nature of thought may not be applicable in an analysis of the nature of social activity.

Social Context

The social situation is defined by Skinner as one where rein-forcement, usually generalized from other sources, requires the medi-ation of another organism. This reinforcement differs from mechani-cal reinforcement in that it may vary more often from moment to moment and thereby create a greater flexibility of response in the organism. Different reinforcements may achieve the same behavioral result, and the same reinforcement may yield different responses on different occasions. Leaders and followers develop in the social situation where a division of labor is necessary. The leader is under the control of external variables, and the follower is under the control of variables associated with the leader. Love, friendship, etc., are analyzed as the mutual tendencies of two or more individuals to administer positive reinforcement to one another. Skinner's analysis ends here, or rather, becomes more complex only in terms of the reinforcement involved. There is no attempt to look within the structure of the organism for an answer to questions such as "Why in the first place do any given two people want to reinforce one another to the exclusion of a third or fourth party?"

Ethics as usually conceived in their religious and philosophic sense are not approachable through a behavioral system. One can, however, initiate procedures through behavioral engineering which will maximize the probability that an individual will behave in a way consistent with a given ethical system. This is another matter. Although Skinner does not specifically so state, it seems fairly certain that he has little patience with attempts to justify a given ethical system *a priori*. One has the impression from a reading of *Walden II* (Skinner, 1948) that the "good" will somehow be a product of constant behavioral experimentation. An alternative within this behavioral context is to forget about ethics and the "good" as meaningful concepts altogether.

The concept of "responsibility" suffers a similar fate. For Skinner, what one means when he speaks of responsibility, usually a social concept, is that rewards and punishments have been associated with various forms of behavior, verbal or otherwise. These are the forms of behavior which have emerged as important ones for society as a whole. They are usually connected with life, death, and property.

A society, through the form of power known as its governmental agencies, will be interpreted as free by its constituents if it maximizes the use of positive reinforcements in its exercise of control. The citizen, however, is just as much controlled as if he lived in a dictatorship emphasizing punishment as a controlling device. A completely "free" society is one in which the individual is controlled by other than governmental agencies.

Since we have been concerned with the assumptions and methodology of Skinner's functional approach to understanding human activity, it might be profitable to examine briefly its limits of explanatory possibility. If we conceive of human behavior as continuous along a dimension of complexity of the reinforcers and operants which form the core of behavior, then at the simple pole of the scale the question of why an operant is reinforceable in the first place is answered by referring to the evolutionary history of the organism. The fact that operant reinforcement takes place in organisms is undeniable. However, the reason that responses followed by reinforcers lead to an increased probability that the responses will be forthcoming in similar future situations is to be found in the nature of the development of the species over evolutionary time. On several occasions in *Science and Human Behavior,* Skinner refers to the evolutionary history of the species as perhaps the most profitable area in which to examine the question of why emotional or aversive responses are elicited by the organism at all. The origins of the functional relationships in organisms are to be found in the biology and eventually in the chemistry and physics of the species. The question of whether it would be immediately fruitful to concentrate our efforts on those reductions with respect to human behavior will be raised in the final chapter of this book.

At the complex pole of the operant scale, the limitations of the system seem to lie in the *a priori* characteristics of the human thought process suggested by Kant. This is not to suggest that Kant's conception of the *a priori* is necessarily relevant to modern science, or functional-reductive theories in particular. Kant introduces the possibility of the existence of some type of *a priori* knowledge, in contrast to the skeptical position of Hume. As we have mentioned, Hume also recognized the necessity of some reference to the *a priori* in epistemology, but was more taken with his contingency analysis, especially regarding the nature of causality. These *a priori* characteristics too, presumably beyond the reach of the verbal operant, may best be understood in evolutionary terms. Should this be the case, Skinner's behavioral analysis is restricted and perhaps transitory. Once these evolutionary processes are discovered, the functions among variables yielded by behavioral analysis may have only immediate practical value and be less efficient than a biologically oriented explanation of the same phenomena. On the other hand, if it is unreasonable to suggest that all complex thought can be explained by either behavioral analysis or biological study, the unit of explanation shifts to the nature of the concepts involved in thought processes. Failing satisfactory explanation here, we may be truly stymied.

Helson's Adaptation-level Theory

A theorist who is not ordinarily associated with social psychology has recently formalized the concept of adaptation level to explain behavior ranging from the psychophysical judgment to social affiliation. Helson differs from Skinner in recognizing the necessity of clearly stating the assumptions and postulates of his approach. Unlike Skinner, he favors an attempt to build a specific theoretical structure through which to study various forms of behavior. On the other hand, both theorists are alike in that the core of their system depends heavily upon the functional relationship between independent and dependent variables. As we shall see, Helson is not averse to suggesting the use of hypothetical explanatory concepts to aid theorizing.

Central to the concept of adaptation is the idea that the organism seeks to adjust to its environment by maintaining an equilibrium between internal and external conditions. The term "adaptation" has been used in biology and implies that the organism has native equipment which operates to optimize physiological or behavioral responses under varying internal and external conditions. It is obvious that the use of a concept such as adaptation requires an inference to a non-observed entity or process. That is, we infer an adaptive mechanism from physiological or behavioral activities which seem to produce equilibrium along some physiological or psychological dimension. This is especially true when behavioral processes are involved. For example, we may observe an animal attempt to minimize his amount of general activity when he has been forced to perform for long periods of time on an activity wheel. Conversely, the same animal will seek activity on the same wheel when his access to it has been preceded by long periods of inactivity in a cramped space. Since Helson centers his analysis of human behavior on such a concept as adaptation, the difference between his and Skinner's systems is readily seen.

Although Helson carefully distinguishes among various types of adaptation, such as homeostasis, sensory adaptation, motor adaptation, and behavioral adaptation, the general concept underlying all of these subdivisions remains the same. There is a tendency on the part of animal organisms to react to internal and external stimuli so as to maintain or restore an equilibrium and thus to maximize the probability that the animal will survive. The tendency may be behavioral or directly physiological. It may involve a specific body part, such as the stomach or liver, or it may be concerned with processes where underlying bodily structures are not or cannot be specified. Mechanisms exist for maintaining and restoring fixed values of physical and chemical constants associated with vital bodily processes, as well as for maintaining and restoring peaceful relations between groups, classes and nations.

Thinking is a form of behavior. Laws of logic rest on actual and possible forms of behavior, the latter occurring only in thought. Hence, through behavioral analysis it is possible to understand what it means to think and to exercise logic. These cognitive processes obey laws that have a formal structure similar to that of laws involving sensory, perceptual, and judgmental phenomena. It follows from our earlier discussion that cognitive processes contribute to the adaptation of the organism to his environment, a point made by Helson. From the hypothesis that adaptation is a process common to many aspects of behavior, it follows that only the *form* of behavioral laws governing thought processes are reducible to, or are the same as, the form of laws governing less complex behavior. This does not imply that cognition is totally reducible to sensation, a more fundamental

form of behavior, although eventually it may be empirically demonstrated that explanation of cognitive behavior is, in fact, reducible
to explanation of sensation or perception or some other basic kind
of behavior.

In examining interpersonal behavior and the nature of groups,
Helson accepts the notion that groups display properties which are
not reducible to the tenets of individual behavior. However, an emphasis on the behavior of individuals in groups remains the central
idea of social psychology. What does it mean for a group to exhibit
a characteristic that is not reducible to functional contingencies associated with individual behavior? To answer this we must first examine
the group characteristics themselves. Helson lists four:

    1. The actions and goals of groups are more than the sum of the
actions and goals of the individuals composing them.
    2. Groups persist although their individual units change.
    3. There is interaction among the members of groups, the degree of
which determines the strength or cohesion of the whole.
    4. Groups respond as wholes to the stimuli directed to their parts
(1964, pp. 584-5).

These properties occur only if there is communication among the
members of the group. Although group characteristics are recognized,
they are thought to be products of interacting individuals. Explanation about them is ultimately reducible to explanation about the behavior of individuals. Much may be learned about group behavior
from their "natural units," that is, units involving interaction among
individual members. According to the first characteristic of groups,
Helson believes that groups have properties not equivalent to the
sum of their individual members. He also believes that explanation
of group behavior is ultimately reducible to explanation of individual
behavior. This is not necessarily a contradiction. This means that the
singular element in the group behavior is the activity of individuals,
an activity which is produced only in social situations where individuals interact with one another.

Helson assumes the existence of a mechanism of adaptation in
the organism, but does not specify its character or location at any
given level of structure or function. Adaptation or adjustment is a

fundamental fact of social as well as individual behavior, and the stimulus characteristics occurring in group situations can be classified in a manner similar to stimuli relevant to individual behavior. The adaptation level of the group is characterized by specifying the conditions under which the group divides equally, remains indifferent, or divides unequally with respect to various alternatives on any given issue. The stimuli involved in such a characterization, however, are more complex than those associated with psychophysics, for example. They may have "demand characteristics." As well as being simply stimuli in the particular social episode (for example, a group deciding whether to go to the movies or to the opera), individuals also interact as friendly, hostile, boring, etc. Helson speaks of a "reality dimension" in social behavior which is not relevant to the psychophysical situation. One may feel that an adaptation approach to social behavior contributes some information as to its qualities but is not capable of dealing with "reality dimensions" or "demand characteristics" of stimuli in the social situation. We have an indication from Helson's own words of caution that what we ordinarily conceive of as the social situation or social behavior will not be explained totally by the concept of adaptation-level. The question now becomes what will be explained by using Helson's approach?

The empirical studies described by Helson largely involve the pooling of physical and other stimuli with the social background characteristics of the subjects, conformity and social pressure phenomena, and assimilation and contrast of social stimuli. In social conformity and in situations where there are assimilation and contrast effects regarding such social phenomena as opinion or attitude, the concept of equilibrium, and therefore of adaptation as described by Helson, seem to work. There are social pressures exerted in the form of threats, coercions, and rewards which insure conformity in many, perhaps most, social situations, and insure apparent non-conformity or rebellion in others. To discover the functional relationships among the many variables which are concomitant with these phenomena is undoubtedly useful. Contrast and assimilation in opinion and attitude phenomena also seem to be responses that fluctuate around some equilibrious center. However, the general concept of adaptation does not aid our further understanding of the structure of these phenomena, any more than the equilibrious concepts of drive, ego or homeostasis aid in understanding the nature of learning, motivation, etc. As a general concept, adaptation may have merit as a crude approximation of a solution. That is, certain forms of higher-level thinking, such as solving a scientific problem or writing a novel, seem to have no equilibrious pattern. The individual continues to work at his self-structured task without displaying the cyclical activity usually seen in other types of tasks, such as eating or sleeping.

Examples of Functional-Nonreductive and Fractionated Theories

In the approach of Skinner, and of many other social behavior theorists, emphasis is placed upon the idea of reinforcement. For theorists who favor other than a completely functional point of view, learning theory has played a central part in their attempts to understand social behavior. When these theories have relied mainly on learning principles gathered from research on animals and individual behavior, they have failed, in many instances, to handle adequately all or most of the data available to psychologists. Bandura and Walters (1963) have taken the position that an understanding of human social behavior can be gained only from situations where the basic empirical information is gathered in dyadic and group situations. Their method is functional, but nonreductive. They point out that any reinforcement theory has great difficulty in explaining novel responses. (For Skinner, a selective reinforcement of certain responses in an individual's vast repertoire produces gradually evolved novel responses.) Furthermore, much social learning seems to occur through the process of imitation where there is no possibility that the behavior could have been reinforced by the individual who is the model. Thus there is some evidence that reinforcement is not necessary for learning.

If imitation, whereby the child acquires responses *in toto* from adults, does occur in a variety of situations, then the social act itself, without reduction to individual elements of behavior, becomes a basic unit for understanding many social activities. The verbal exchange between two or more individuals is also a source of imitative behavior, and some aspects of language may have meaning only as a set of conventions within the social context. Note that all of this is behavior and readily observable to the qualified individual.

Aside from the approaches presented above, there are few attempts to explain or predict all of social behavior within the behavior theory framework. The theorists are themselves cautious in estimating the amount and type of social behavior which could fall under the rubric of their respective systems. Many of the followers of Clark L. Hull have written theories about social behavior, including analyses of social drives, emotion, learning, etc. Aside from our brief comments on imitation, we have given this approach little space because its assumptions are the same as those in some of the systems we have already discussed. Theorists of this persuasion generally are not concerned with all of social behavior. In fact, most modern American theorizing regarding social behavior is fractionated to the extent that theorists concentrate on problems involving a single aspect of social behavior to the exclusion, at least temporarily, of other aspects. There are behavioral theories of leadership, social motivation, attitude organization and change, problem solving in small groups, and a host of others. Usually the theorist takes pains to emphasize that the principles of his theory are not necessarily relevant to another aspect of social activity. By far the greatest number of systems of explanation in social psychology today are of this type. If we compare these fractionated systems with complete systems, we get an interesting but perhaps expected result. The fractionated systems are less reductive than the complete ones. That is, referring once again to our reductive continuum, there is no mention, nor any particular implication, that the fundamental properties and assumptions of the system are ultimately reducible to biological or physical variables. There is less need to do so since the systems, being concerned with only one aspect of social activity, are by definition incomplete. Some examples of these systems follow.

In offering a contingency model of leadership effectiveness, Fiedler (1963) begins with the personality attributes of the leader and their relation to group performance. The personality characteristics comprise some of the elementary units in his system. He assumes that they are one of the principal, nonreducible entities on which a system of explanation regarding leadership in social situations can be built. Other terms of the system involve measurable relationships between the leader and the members of the group, such as the power and authority the leader's position provides, and his personal relations with the members of the group. The various aspects of personality characteristics and leader-follower relationships generally are tapped by structured questionnaires, interviews, or sociograms.

McGuire (1960) has discussed an "inoculation" approach for inducing resistance to persuasion. He combines biological analogy with cognitive organization. Resistance to persuasion is considered to be analogous to medical inoculation against disease. By introducing a weak strain of disease germs into the body, relevant bodily processes are mobilized to eliminate the destructive power of the disease germs. In the mobilization, the bodily processes are permanently, or for a long period of time, capable of dealing effectively with germs which may be introduced later in even stronger doses. To transfer the biological analogy to resistance to persuasion, certain pretreatments can make the subject resistant to changing his opinions, attitudes or beliefs concerning topics which he strongly holds, assuming that the subject is practiced and motivated to defend his position. Although its form is derived from biology, McGuire's theory is involved with an examination of highly complex verbal and motivational factors operating in the organism. In his research, as well as in that of many others in the opinion-attitude area, the materials presented to the subjects, and also the dependent variables, are usually of a verbal, hence cognitive, nature. The studies begin with an attempt to tap an individual opinion or attitude on a certain topic. Most pretreatments involve review of attitudinal material and arguments on the part of the subject. The inoculation theory begins with the assumption that attitudes are already existent and thought processes, such as reasoning, already available to the subject. Hence, even though the form of the theory is a biological analogy, we would be hard pressed to conclude that the theory itself is reductive in nature. The fundamental units involved, such as attitude and all that is implied by thought, may or may not be reduced to other concepts. It is simply not the nature of fractionated theories to deal with this problem.

In summary, aside from theories associated with the origins and formation of social motivation and learned responses, functional-reductive analyses of social activity are relatively rare in current psychological theorizing. Theories associated with social motivation or learning, such as the theories of Skinner (1953) or Helson (1964), usually have similar assumptive bases. The majority of social psychological theories follows a pattern to which we turn in the next chapter.

Summary Chart of the Status of Principal Functional-Reductive Theories on Assumptive Characteristics Relevant to Social Activity

ASSUMPTION	THEORY	
	B. F. Skinner (Operant Conditioning)	H. Helson (Adaptation-Level Theory)
REDUCTION OF PRINCIPAL CONCEPTS	Yes	Yes—For form of explanatory concepts No—For linking of all phenomena under a single set of explanatory concepts
CAUSALITY	Functional—contingency Tradition—Hume	Functional—contingency Tradition—Hume
GENERAL METHODOLOGY	Predictions of clearly defined responses from steady state in organism, input-output focus	Predictions of clearly defined responses connected to hypothetical entities of specific theory
USE OF STATISTICS	Minimal use—opposed conceptually Experimental control maximized	Moderate use—no conceptual opposition
RESEARCH TIME PERSPECTIVE	Historical	Historical

chapter

5

Holistic Theories

If one were to ask a modern psychologist to list as many theories or systems of social psychology as he could, it is highly likely that more of those named would be found in this chapter than in any of the others. The systems of Lewin, Asch, Krech and Crutchfield, and Newcomb would undoubtedly be among the first listed. Some of the central ideas descend in a rather direct line from Kant, through Husserl, Brentano, von Ehrenfels and others, to the gestalt theorists of the early part of this century. This is not to say that all of the men listed are Kantians, but rather that a way of thinking is common to all of them, whatever other important divergences may be present. I shall not discuss the phenomenologists, but rather begin with one culmination of that approach, namely, the gestalt psychology of Wertheimer, Koffka and Kohler.

Since our study is comparative, some mention of the juxtaposition of behaviorism and gestalt is appropriate here. The two systems were, as every psychologist knows, in a kind of opposition to one another in the twenties and thirties of this century. The competition flared briefly and then died. Both general approaches left much to be desired, and many of the apparent conflicts turned out to be apparent and not real. Although the contrasts existing between the two approaches tend to be ignored by today's theorists, there were and are differences that permeate psychology, especially in areas like social psychology where more than one individual is needed to form a fundamental unit of study. There are still at least two major ways of approaching the study of human activity, and they are exemplified by the early gestalt-behaviorism opposition. From the time of the metaphysical controversy between Hume and Kant to the present, a dichotomy of approach to understanding human activity developed. Clearly, Kant was not disposed to reject the wisdom of learning about human beings and other phenomena through the collection of facts by controlled observation. However, he believed that the very nature of man's thought process ordered and made collective sense out of such observations. As we have seen, Hume was disposed toward this way of thinking but never articulated it as did Kant. Their disciples, wittingly or unwittingly, separated the thinking of the two philosophers over the next two centuries, sharpening their differences and making possible two separate and distinct views of man's nature other than that envisioned by Hume and Kant. Some thinkers, influenced by Hume's ideas, were to emphasize the essentially non-metaphysical nature of all learning and the possibility of reducing all knowledge to a number of basic principles. These principles presumably would define man's essential nature, and the essential nature of all other natural phenomena as well. Nineteenth-century philosophers of science eventually gravitated to some form of this view. Others, following Kant's emphasis, tended to preserve the central position of the total organism as the author of all attempts to order the universe. Man's processes, of *necessity,* could not be reduced to principles separate from his nature. We have examined the fruits of the development from Hume's principal contribution. Those deriving from Kant must be examined next. I will refer particularly to the work of Kurt Koffka (1935), one of the most definitive on the nature of gestalt theory.

Basic Gestalt Assumptions

For gestalt psychology, knowledge, and therefore science, is unitary, although its methods of analysis sometimes result in an apparent destruction of such traditional unitary concepts as God, soul, and personality. The concept of mind, interpreted as a totality, is not rejected as it often is in contemporary psychology and science in general. However, its existence apart from material elements is rejected. Neither mind nor matter is eliminated from consideration. From nature and life, quantity and order are extracted, while from mind, meaning or significance. One may form the idea from this statement that mensurative activities of psychology can be made meaningful only through a unifying principle which allows one to understand fully the measurements involved, while providing a way in which one may gather new measurements concerning the same phenomenon. Obviously, the validity of this position lies in a successful interpretation of what it means for an idea to be meaningful. For the moment we may put this question aside. Unifying principles quite often are statements of qualitative entities before they give way to quantitative expression. This has been true in mathematics and physics, and it is especially true about twentieth-century psychology. If qualitative descriptions are correct, quantitative terms derived from them will be possible at some later time. Gestalt psychology was to be a wedding of the partially successful, quantitative scientific tradition and an older tradition which insisted that life was ordered and not the accidental product of unrelated contingencies. It was to be a science of man in the twentieth century which would utilize the new scientific techniques without losing sight of the old, but valid, problems of metaphysics. Setting forth this credo, Koffka (1935, p. 17 ff) thus set the tone of what has been one of the principal emphases of gestalt, namely, that interaction among many psychological elements is of central importance in understanding human activity. The question then became, how can a fusion take place between the quantitative causal prediction of science and the insistence on grasping meaning as fundamental knowledge emphasized by traditional metaphysics? Koffka attributes the beginning of an answer to Max Wertheimer.

Prediction on the one hand, and meaning or understanding on the other, are not incompatible. They must, in fact, be used as part of one unitary explanation. Hence, the causal connection is not merely an often repeated sequence of otherwise unconnected events, but rather, a connection which is to be understood by some principle beyond it and from which it can be derived. We find that the gestalt position regarding causation is similar to Kant's and inconsistent with that of modern behaviorists. Koffka (1935), however, denies Kantian *a priorism* in favor of the idea that the principles of the perception of objects are isomorphic with the principles of the behavior of the physical things themselves. That is, the laws of organization of the processes of physical entities and the laws of organization of the processes of the behavioral field (see below) are unitary. The task of gestalt psychology is to discover the functional units or wholes, composed of separate facts, which would constitute the full explanation of any phenomenon. The task is narrowed by concentrating on the various *gestalten* of which, presumably, the human mind is composed. The portion of meaning contained in mind is manifest to a greater degree than in any other part of the universe. Although the physicist knows that the sounds composing the symphony he is listening to are all analyzable in terms of waves, he still seeks to enjoy the piece on a different level, that is, holistically. Presumably, gestalt psychology attempts to fuse science and life the way they are not fused in physics, mathematics, or other scientific disciplines.

Gestalt psychology is concerned with behavior, but not in the sense in which the term is usually used by traditional behaviorists. As we have seen, the ultimate solution for the behaviorist lies in the eventual reduction of behavioral terms to those of physiology and similar disciplines. For the gestalt psychologist, the observed behavioral event (called "molar behavior") is the unit of study itself. It is not reducible necessarily to other terms for its full explanation. Explanation, and therefore meaning, exists at the level of overt behavior as we see it in daily life; for example, in a student's attendance at class, a lecturer's delivery, or a pilot's navigation. Gestalt psychology begins and ends with molar behavior. Because it is a nonreductive approach to understanding human activity, the more complex types of human activity such as thinking, loving and enjoying are more easily incorporated within its terms than within the terms of behaviorism. This does not mean that the gestalt approach is necessarily more correct than other systems in explaining these complex activities. One needs to exercise some caution at this point. As observed previously, gestalters assume that all knowledge is unitary; that is, that the meaning contained in the various subdisciplines of science and philosophy are interconnected. The manner and extent of connection are not specified. If the subject matter of psychology is unique, as it must be under the gestalt assumptions, where and how does it fit into their unitary conception of knowledge? The answer would be easily given by behaviorist theories, which expect reduction of all terms over time. Gestalt psychology answers that the form of explanation in the various subdisciplines of knowledge is fundamentally the same, and therefore, that one may speak of a unity. The subject matter of these various subdisciplines, however, must each be unique.

The gestalt approach is further delineated by a consideration of what is called the "behavioral environment." Without being too specific, we may define the "behavioral environment" as the prevalent conditions for the organism at the time some behavior takes place. Also distinguished is a "geographical environment," which refers to the stimulus conditions and geographical location of the individual at the time of behavior. "Behavior" is activity which occurs in the behavioral environment. Generally, the "geographical environment" refers to things "as they really are," and the "behavioral environment" to things as they appear to us. It therefore follows that aspects of the human mind not only mediate between the external stimulus conditions of the environment and behavior, but also shape much if not all of what we perceive as the nature of the pure geographical environment. It also follows that all data are behavioral data since they are part of the behavioral environment, and that "physical reality" is a construction from behavioral data. This point is the same as Mach's concerning the nature of scientific data (discussed above), although it begins from a somewhat different focus. It is a point which behavior theorists made little use of, but that gestalt theorists concentrated upon.

Arising at this stage of the discussion is the Kantian problem of the *"ding an sich."* How do we know real behavior or real objects or events of any kind since we have knowledge only of our behavioral environment? The gestalt answer is that we must assume the existence of real behavior, objects, and events. This explicit assumption is usually not made in behaviorally oriented theories, where, in actuality, it must be held with equal necessity. When an event which is apparently the behavior of another organism occurs within an individual's behavioral environment, he infers the nature of the organism's real behavior. In so doing, the observer is behaving himself, and he has knowledge of this behavior. The individual has included as part of his behavioral environment the activity of the other organism and he himself is part of that environment. This is always true. There is inference to objects and events within the behavioral environment and to the characteristics and activities of the individual which interacts with them. This total pattern of activity is called the "direct experience of consciousness."

From modern physics, gestalt theory takes the concept of the active field as a dynamic interplay of forces. The behavioral environment is assumed to have the properties of a psychological field that is analogous to a physical field of force. The principal attribute of a field, physical or psychological, is that activity, that is, force at any one point in the field, affects all other points since all are in dynamic interaction with one another. The term "force" is taken to have a meaning regarding behavior analogous to that in physics regarding motion. The problem for psychology becomes the determination of a given field at a given time, and of behavior resulting from that field. Human dynamic field properties consist principally of desires, motives, frustrations, avoidances, etc. (as these terms are usually used in everyday language), associated with various objects and events in an individual's life. Objects and events push and pull the individual in many directions, towards and away from other objects and events. However, the behavioral environment is not identical with the psychological field. There are many reasons for this, but it suffices to say that one is the active principle (field) found in the other. All activity including reflexive and physiological responses is field determined in some way. This principle is taken to be universal within the gestalt system. We can only assume that objects and events around us have the characteristics and activities we think they do. The field notion is not necessarily a property of these objects and events, but a way of examining them.

It is now possible to utilize two assumptions:

1. The existence of nonreducible molar behavior.
2. That behavioral, in fact, all processes having field or inter-active properties, or being best understood by reference to these properties, may be used as explanatory devices.

Gestalters admit that all psychological processes, whether part of the behavioral environment or part of the reflexive system of the organism, are ultimately products of the organism's physiology. This implies a reduction of behavioral terms to physiological ones and seems to contradict an earlier statement that gestalt theory assumed the nonreducibility of behavioral events. The problem is solved presumably by the introduction of the concept of molar physiological processes existing in an isomorphic relationship to molar behavioral events. The evidence for the existence of molar physiological events rests mainly on the general observation that in chemistry and physics, for example, there is no simple additive relationship when two or more elements combine, but an entirely new product, as when hydrogen ions combine with oxygen ions to form water. It is possible that the physiology of the central nervous system functions in much the same integrative manner, rather than as an additive system of separate and distinct neuron firings which, as a result of stimulation, summate to produce various patterns of behavior. If such molar nerve activity does occur, it might correspond one to one with a complex, integrative behavioral response pattern of the kind already cited. A kind of reduction to physiology would be achieved without sacrificing the utilization of a total behavior pattern (*gestalten*) as the most advantageous unit of study. Hence, there may be many kinds of physiological processes corresponding to the many behavioral patterns with which we are becoming familiar. The implication is that each local physiological nerve process depends on all other local physiological nerve processes within a given molar distribution and, ultimately, on activity in the entire nervous system. The one-to-one relationship existing between the physiological molar processes as cause and the behavioral molar processes as effect is called "isomorphism." Gestalt theorists conclude that it is possible therefore to utilize molar psychological observations as material for physiological theory. Since all observation consists of observation of the behavioral facts of direct experience, there exists the possibility of learning about the physiological processes from behavioral ones. This same contention was made by Ernst Mach in his *Analysis of Sensations,* discussed above. We have noted that Mach gave impetus not only to this gestalt idea, but also to part of the fundamental position of behaviorism which insists that the objective measurement of stimuli and responses (sights, sounds, etc.) constitutes the basic data of psychological science. We have seen how this analysis can be performed with the geographical environment. The step to the physiological environment has the same logical status.

The final form of the assumption may be stated as follows: Conscious (direct) experience is coupled with its corresponding physiological process and has essentially the same structural properties. The structural properties consist of the form of activity found in the physical processes of the brain and the form of activity found in thought or other types of mental activity. One may preserve a molar level of analysis and, at the same time, retain physiological observations which are relevant to any analysis of behavior. Thus, gestalt theory is ultimately a theory of physiology.

Koffka is very careful to point out that although gestalt theory is essentially a physiological one, it cannot be so completely. "The physiological processes which we construct as the correlates of consciousness *are known to us in the first place through their conscious aspect"* (Koffka, 1935, p. 65; italics Lana's). Thus, whatever the conditions of consciousness may be, knowledge of them necessarily precedes any conclusions regarding physiology, behavior, or the isomorphic relations between them. Koffka recognizes that consciousness does not enter into his system of explanation. It seems that in the gestalt system conscious processes have the character of an *a priori* which is recognized as preceding the system, although perhaps Koffka would deny this contention (Koffka, 1935, pp. 305 &

549). This conceptual position places gestalt theory in a strange kinship with behaviorism. Both systems skirt the initial problems of consciousness which, for systems that purport to have a scientific bias, is absolutely necessary. The kinship suggests that neither system is more sophisticated in terms of the validity of certain initial assumptions. It is true that gestalt theorists, at least in the past, seemed to recognize their assumptive bases more readily than behavior theorists.

Having established the isomorphic connection between physiological and behavioral activity, it becomes possible to make conclusions about physiology from the more accessible data of behavior. The task of psychology becomes the study of behavior in its causal connection with the psychophysical (geographical and physiological) field. It is important to note that, since the molar, or "field," nature of physiological activity is a construct originating from behavioral observation, the initial inferential direction of gestalt theory is from observed behavior to physiology.

Although gestalt theory has concentrated mainly upon the study of visual perception, it is worthwhile to examine some of the early gestalt thinking regarding social, that is, group, behavior. Consistent with their initial assumptions, gestalters believe that group behavior of human beings involves reaction patterns which are specific only to group situations. These patterns constitute a group gestalt. That is, the various parts (members) are interdependent, and they should be analyzed as such. The cohesion of the group is the same as the strength of its gestalt character. The group follows gestalt principles of individual behavior, and its sociological characteristics can be explained by, or reduced to, these principles of individual behavior. An individual provides stimulation within another individual's behavioral field, as any other object might. With this orientation, the individual operating within the group situation is preserved as a relatively independent functioning unit. It is his behavioral environment which is influenced by the reality of the sociological group situation. Thus, an entire foundation of a social psychology exists in the gestalt psychology of the individual. One need only substitute human beings for other objects within the behavioral field. It remained for Kurt Lewin to give the gestalt interpretation of social behavior its most sophisticated expression.

Lewin

Lewin believed that psychology was most likely not re-ducible in all of its elements to physics. He felt reasonably assured that there was a separate science of interpersonal relations, that is, social psychology. He attributed psychological reductionism (to the terms and laws of physics) to certain misconceptions concerning the nature of science. These misconceptions were found in a major por-tion of the history of philosophy and science throughout the past two thousand years. One great difficulty, he felt, was the enormous emphasis placed on the history of the appropriate unit under exami-nation. Historicity refers to the dependence upon evidence consti-tuted by the repetition of an event over time to support a particular hypothesis which in turn is part of the structure of a theory. Lewin contended that modern physics, unlike pre-Galilean physics, no longer depends upon this type of evidence, but upon evidence gathered in the immediate "field" environment of the unit or units under study. From these initial comments it should seem apparent that Lewin depends upon the structure of theory in physics as a guide to that in psychology. He uses physical and mathematical examples and references throughout the formation of the terms and units of his system. However, it would be misleading to put too great an emphasis on this. The roots of Lewin's system go deeper than mod-ern physics, both historically and conceptually. He utilized these terms largely because they were the first available to indicate that the em-phasis of study was to be on a total pattern of environmental condi-tions at a particular point or in a particular segment of time. The emphasis of study was not to be on the histories of the various events involved, or on the relevant developmental processes leading to the time when the events were studied. A conclusion dependent upon a series of observed, historical antecedents whose only connection is their similarity and, perhaps, closeness in time, can yield only limited information. The really important conclusions to be made about any phenomena, particularly those involving human beings, are yielded by study of the vast, relevant complex of internal and external oc-currences present at the time the event-to-be-explained takes place.

It is interesting that both Lewin and Skinner reject the usefulness of repetitive frequency in experiment as the *sine qua non* for the
possibility of generalizing phenomena from the experiment to the
natural conditions of the organism. Both do so on different, although
not mutually exclusive, grounds. Skinner insists upon careful control of factors affecting the individual organism in a given experimental setting. Lewin insists upon being aware of all the relevant
factors impinging upon the organism at the time an observation is
made. At this point Lewin, as had his gestalt colleagues, wished to
introduce into his psychology the concept of meaning. For Lewin,
and other gestalt psychologists, meaning was predicated upon the
gestalt configuration present in any given situation. In order to understand why an individual suddenly breaks down in a fit of hysterical
weeping in the middle of a social evening, one must know what the
perceptions of that individual were with respect to the various guests
and the hosts; the context of "party"; the individual's perception at
that moment; etc. The event may never occur again, but an understanding of it may be extremely important in understanding the
person involved and in predicting future behavior.

It follows from this that the concept of experiment must also
be modified. Repetition as the *sine qua non* for successful experimental conclusions must be given less importance, if not eliminated
altogether. Experiments must attempt to recreate, or structure in the
first place, an environmental situation which reproduces some aspect
of the normal pattern of living of the individual involved. Under
these conditions the dynamic relationships inherent in such a pattern
may become apparent. The concrete case must be the raw material
from which laws and theories are eventually constructed and tested.
Statistical numerosity associated with a small bit of behavior may be
useful in certain situations, but it can never yield answers to the important questions about human beings.

There has been much criticism of an ahistorical emphasis in
Lewin's formation of psychological laws, especially by the Yale-Iowa
group. Without reviewing the various criticisms, we shall indicate
certain problems which are inherent in this aspect of Lewin's assumptive base. Most behaviorists, and indeed most scientists, would

argue that in using an historical approach they are attempting to understand a given aspect of behavior (or activity, in the case of inorganic subject matter) in the most complete way possible. A separate question, which Lewin apparently does not isolate from the principal one, is whether it is possible to use an historical approach in addition to his own. It becomes clearer if we isolate Lewin's two propositions, the first concerning the impossibility of understanding phenomena through historical repetition of events, and the second insisting upon the analysis of an event within its natural context. All scientists perhaps would accept the validity of the second proposition, while many would reject the validity of the first. Behavioristically oriented psychologists have accepted the proposition that organisms are ultimately to be understood in their natural context. Yet, they are committed to the *methodological* position that observation of repeated events in the history of an organism, occurring under controlled conditions, is the best road to understanding. The question becomes, how does Lewin intend to structure non-historical psychological research? This, of course, is a methodological question. Lewin takes his model from field physics and vector analysis which depend upon the mutual relations of several physical facts and are non-historical. Thus Lewin describes "psychological vectors" as movements (literal or figurative) towards or away from objects (literal or figurative) in the individual's environment. He chose vector concepts from physics to supply a concrete model for the psychological field situation, a model which preserves emphasis on all the forces operating at a given time on a given individual and which focuses on the concrete ahistorical situation. Whether or not the structure of vector analysis or field physics is used consistently by Lewin is really irrelevant to his intent. Behaviorists have also used loosely fitting physical and mathematical models in the past with no great damage to the validity of their systems on that account.

Lewin had to depend heavily upon the single demonstration or case (the *experimentum crucis* of the gestalt psychology of perception) in understanding human social activity. For Lewin, connections among events are never causes of other events. We are dealing with events in a psychic field, rather than in a physical environment (in the manner, discussed above, of gestalt psychology in general). Each concrete case must be examined to discover from where the "causal energies" that determine such a "psychical event" arise.

In Chapter Two, a type of causation was discussed whereby a series of antecedent and current events mutually influenced one another and produced a series of other events. The example was the single billiard ball striking many others, which in turn strike others, until a pattern of ball responses develops. Observation of the various paths resulting from the collision of the balls was necessary to make sense of the particular pattern of action on the billiard table at that time. The observation could tell us about the pattern of movement of all the balls only after the initial collision had occurred. Induction to the future had no place in the process. However, inference to unobserved times is possible. One could indicate that other balls on another table at another time probably would follow the same field principles of interaction discovered in the first instance. In this case, even though it is logically possible to disentangle the various "field" lines of causation attributable to the action of each ball, the over-all pattern of reaction may be more meaningful to the observer. The same would be true of the process of causation inherent in Lewin's psychological field situation.

Whatever Lewin's full intent may have been in using an ahistorical epistemological concept, he ultimately emphasized interactive causation as the necessary as well as most meaningful conceptualization for psychology of cause and effect. Certainly, he did not mean to minimize the past history of the organism with respect to the behavior to be explained. That he embraced the drive concept of necessity implied the recognition of a relevant history of conditions giving rise to the drive. He also accepted equilibrium, the end state following the removal of drive in the organism, as a meaningful concept, but only for the system as a whole.

The final point in our discussion of Lewin concerns his approach to experimentation, which emphasizes the total environmental situation. This is contrasted to the type of psychological research which gathers historical-statistical data relative to a particular segmented problem of human behavior. One finds here the weakest link in Lewin's system. Up to this point, Lewin had succeeded in criticizing the connectionist behavioral approach. He did this in a manner derived from Kant's theory of causality which, in turn, had successfully criticized Hume's continuity theory of causality, at least as far as Hume had developed it. Lewin lists a series of experimental results which are taken to support various contentions derived from Lewinian field theory. However, the conditions under which the experiments were performed are no different from those used by theorists supporting an historical, behavioristic epistemology and methodology. For example, Lewin cites a study by Mahler (1933) on substitute activities of differing degrees of reality in which different tasks (thinking, talking, actual doing) are substituted for various uncompleted tasks. In the reporting of results, the number of tasks not completed, and the number completed by substitution, were tallied under varying circumstances, in much the same manner as one would do were he concerned with a conclusion based upon the frequency of an event in time. Again, in a study by Zeigarnik (1927), arithmetical means of various subject responses were used to demonstrate the validity of several theoretical points. Lewin's interpretation of these and other experiments is consistent with his field assumptions, but the structure of many of the studies differs little from those performed by theorists of radically different theoretical persuasions. It is important to maintain a meaningful connection between a theoretical position and the research used to support it. It is also important to maintain a relatively inclusive theoretical position, without allowing it to be reduced to a set of postulates regarding isolated, fragmented problems. Lewin accepted the hereditary challenge derived from Kant and Hume, met it head on in theory, but failed somehow to do likewise in experiment. However, he recognized most of the theoretical problems and started social psychologists thinking along a dimension from which they as yet have not turned.

Perhaps the three most influential attempts to deal with the entire gamut of social psychological problems from the 1940's to the present are those by Krech and Crutchfield, Asch, and Newcomb. The first two works are clearly within the gestalt-field theoretical purview, and the third is very much influenced by it. We shall examine all three works, since they illuminate two major problems in theorizing in social psychology.

Krech and Crutchfield

In a major effort to organize and explain the vast body of social psychological phenomena by a series of clearly stated principles, Krech and Crutchfield utilized the ideas of gestalt field psychology (already reviewed here), with the extensions provided by Kurt Lewin. With the gestalters and Lewin, they assume that there is no theoretical distinction to be drawn between the social field and the non-social field. They submit that the psychologist must study man as a social being in order to understand him at all. This follows from the field position that behavior is best understood when the tensions, motives, etc., operating on the individual at a particular time are discovered. The authors also make the characteristic gestalt assumption that an individual's psychological functioning is no different in social behavior than it is in any other kind of behavior. It is assumed, however, that, within the theoretical context, the explanation of social behavior is not reducible to any explanation of other behavior, although it is continuous with simpler forms of human activity (Krech and Crutchfield, 1948, pp. 30-40). At first glance, these may seem to be contradictory assumptions, but it can be shown that they are not if one takes into account the field-theoretical position. We shall do this in the final chapter.

The theoretical structure of Krech and Crutchfield's system is contained in a series of propositions. These largely are statements regarding characteristics of the psychological field, characteristics of perception, and modes of reorganizing, that is, changing, perception. Propositions about the psychological field include emphasis on the study of molar behavior, rather than of molecular behavior, the necessity for psychological field analysis, tensions in the field leading to change and to more stable structures, and the behavioral modes of the individual under these conditions. Propositions about the perceptual and cognitive processes include the idea of natural structure and organization, functional selectivity, field characteristics, and perceptual contiguity. Propositions about the reorganization of the perceptual cognitive field concern goal blockage which leads to cognitive reorganization and thus to reduction of field tension, hierarchical reorganization, changes in time, and change in the field due to certain characteristics of its original structure.

From these initial principles, Krech and Crutchfield conclude that the process or structure which most nearly includes, in a dynamic, organized manner, all of the relevant perceptual, cognitive phenomena is that which has been labeled "attitude" by social psychologists. Related concepts such as "belief" and "opinion" also have characteristics described within an attitudinal frame of reference. Although the social behavior of the individual is explicable in terms of motivational, emotional, perceptual, and learning processes, "it is neither convenient, nor perhaps possible to describe, analyze, and predict the individual's social behavior by reference to these fundamental processes considered singly" (Krech and Crutchfield, 1948, p. 149). The "perhaps" should have been omitted from the above statement, since behavior is presumably a result of all psychological processes operating simultaneously. The proper unit of analysis is always a "field" unit, one which is *never* reducible to units of individual behavior, even though a social unit such as "attitude" may represent the simultaneous operation of many individual processes including "motive," "perception," and "cognition." We find evidence of indecision on the part of gestalt theorists to reject fully the possibility that a field-derived unit of analysis might be meaningfully reducible to simpler units.

Krech and Crutchfield cite experiments similar (indeed, many are exactly the same) to Lewin's. Compared with Lewin's work, Krech and Crutchfield's lacks an emphasis on the necessity for an ahistorical and, therefore, non-frequency approach to the gathering of experimental evidence.

Asch

Perhaps the purest gestalt experimentation in social psychology is found in the research program of Solomon Asch, who clearly states that his analysis of social behavior uses as its major theoretical foundation the assumptions of gestalt psychology. Although his assumptive base is largely the same as Krech and Crutchfield's, Asch utilizes less formal structure in his analysis, viewing social psychology as an extension of general psychology. He does not believe, however, in the possibility for reduction of psychological events or structures to those in another system such as physiology. Nor does he find it possible to reduce social events to individual events, although he submits that social facts remain part of the psychology of the individual. Asch makes the gestalt field assumption, but he emphasizes that functional analysis is a very important part of social psychology, as is phenomenal analysis from the field situation. Thus, we see a loosening of the restrictions on functional analysis as described by the early gestalters and Kurt Lewin.

In the 1940's and 1950's, Asch did a series of now famous experiments on the influence of social pressure on conformity of judgments in a group situation. Its prototype consists of the following situation. A single subject is made to believe that he is part of a group of eight or nine individuals taking part in an experiment on perceptual judgment. The task might be to estimate the lengths of lines presented to the group, with the group members calling out their estimates. Unknown to the subject, the other members of the group are confederates of the experimenter and will respond with various degrees of obvious misjudgment as to the lengths of the lines. The confederates respond to present consistent agreement, but with such obvious error that the subject should perceive the difference between his judgment and that of the confederates. The problem is to note any change in the subject's successive estimates, as a result of the group consensus and his own incredulity at their estimates. In many experiments the subject responded to the group pressure against his own (better) judgment. His judgment of the lengths of the lines came to conform to the groups'.

This study of Asch's is an excellent example of gestalt-field experimentation. It differs in several ways from behavioristically oriented experimentation, for example. However, there is no logical impediment stopping a behavioristically oriented theorist from doing an Asch type of experiment. The prototype uses only a single subject, so the conditions of the study must be carefully defined and constructed to allow a meaningful conclusion without invoking frequency data to portray an "average" result. Although there are repeated presentations of various line combinations in the experiment, it is not done necessarily to collect an "average" response pattern, but rather to allow the subject's psychological field to develop as he perceives repeatedly the responses of the confederates in the experimental situation. The subject might perceive a single trial as containing an "odd" error. Hence, several trials are needed to form the necessary conditions to test the hypothesis regarding the effects of social influence.

The experiment was followed by a group discussion where the subject's cognitive-emotional perceptions and activities were examined by the experimenter who acted as group leader. Much weight is placed on the subject's subjective reports after the experiment. The experiment stands as a true gestalt-field experimental study, although Asch repeated the study with 31 critical subjects. That is, he felt it necessary to control for individual differences and gather some frequency evidence for his conclusions. Thus, for this modern gestalt social psychological theorist, the earlier insistence on ahistorical data is no longer really feasible. The techniques of gestalt and behaviorist experimentation have combined, at least along certain dimensions. We shall discuss the various methodologies in Chapter Eight.

Newcomb

Certain important elements of Newcomb's (1950; Turner and Converse, 1965) thinking concerning the nature of social psychology are compatible with a general gestalt approach. Clearly, his study of the problems of social behavior is eclectic in that experiments as diverse as those involving conditioning, and those which emphasize the total perceptual organization of a single subject (like Asch's), are used to exemplify the characteristics of many types of social behavior. He makes only a few assumptions and these are made in the form of hypotheses rather than in the form of definitely stated assumptions.

Newcomb focuses upon the various "rules of combination" of psychological states, and the relationship of these states to objects in the world. The one common property of interaction is communication. All individuals existing in these various interactive situations communicate with one another, and this communication therefore becomes the one genre of social psychological research which is related to all others. The property of individuals interacting in groups cannot be reduced to the properties of the individual members when they are not acting as part of a group. As do Krech and Crutchfield, Newcomb believes that the concept of attitude also plays a central role in understanding social behavior. "Attitude," for most theorists, refers to predispositions to act, think, and perceive which have developed under emotional conditions in the life of an individual. The topical core of an attitude almost always involves groups of people classifiable in some way by the individual holding it. Thus, Newcomb is very much concerned with attitude, since his system centers around communicative concepts.

In the systems presented in this chapter, we see a clearly developing tendency to move away from a strict theoretical presentation of social activity as derived from the basic principles of traditional gestalt psychology. However, the influence and the fundamental thinking that we are presenting as the gestalt-field position is evident in the approaches of these theorists. We hope to indicate in Chapters Eight and Nine what seem to be the most fruitful aspects of these theoretical points of view.

As a final illustration of the development of social psychological theorizing as it has been influenced by the Kant-gestalt tradition, it is necessary to mention one theory within the gestalt rubric which is, in a sense, a fragmented one. The various theorists discussed above attempted to integrate the then existing topics contained in all of social psychology. That is, they tried to produce a theory or explanation of social man. Because the problem was seen to be an extremely difficult one, and because certain sub-areas appeared to be central to the understanding of so many others within social psychology,

theories involving social communication, leadership, and the formation and change of attitudes sprang up in the literature. Perhaps the
most important of these sub-areas is the last mentioned.

One of the most recent theories of attitude formation and change
was published by C. W. Sherif, M. Sherif, and R. E. Nebergall
(1965). The authors felt a need for a "disciplined phenomenology
as a basis for theorizing." This mainly involved an assessment of the
degree of involvement and personal commitment of an individual
on some issue. An examination of the authors' major concepts indicates the dependence of the system on the psychological field-type
situation which has been discussed in this chapter. Factors include
the frame of reference of the individual respondent, his ego involvement, and his evaluative categories brought to the attitudinal situation, all of which indicate a focus on units of analysis which are
nonreductive. These factors, attributable to single individuals, operate
in a field-type of network which must be understood to make a meaningful interpretation of attitude formation and change.

Summary Chart of the Status of Principal Holistic Theories on Assumptive Characteristics Relevant to Social Activity

ASSUMPTION	THEORY			
	Gestalt—Koffka	Lewin—Field	Krech and Crutchfield	Asch
REDUCTION OF PRINCIPAL CONCEPTS	Yes—By way of behavioral—physiological isomorphism No—By way of explanation of elements comprising a totality	No	Yes—By way of continuity with the forms of explanation of individual behavior No—By way of explanation of elements comprising a totality	No
CAUSALITY	Productive—(necessity involved) Tradition—Kant	Productive—(necessity involved) Tradition—Kant	Productive—(necessity involved) Tradition—Kant	Productive—(necessity involved) Tradition—Kant
GENERAL METHODOLOGY	Explanation through *experimentum crucis*	Explanation through conceptual (motivational, cognitive, emotional) analysis of immediate behavioral field of group	Essentially same as Lewin	Essentially same as Lewin
USE OF STATISTICS	Minimal use—conceptually opposed	Minimal use—conceptually opposed	Minimal use—less conceptual opposition than Gestalt and Lewin	Minimal use—less conceptual opposition than Gestalt and Lewin
RESEARCH TIME PERSPECTIVE	Ahistorical	Ahistorical	Ahistorical (less strong an emphasis than Gestalt and Lewin)	Ahistorical (less strong an emphasis than Gestalt and

Psychoanalysis and the Instinctive Basis of Social Activity

The influence of Freud and psychoanalysis on the psychology of the past fifty years has been so great that it hardly seems possible to avoid at least some discussion of Freud's theory of social activity within the context of this study. Yet, Freud's position is not particularly recognizable as a theory of social activity when compared with other modern theories on this subject. It is a theory, at least in part, of the essentially immutable characteristics of the developing individual who comes to have a "need" for engaging in group or social activity. This is not to say that Freud used only instincts to explain human behavior. Concepts having to do with the working of the ego and superego, which were not necessarily instinctive in character, were also emphasized. However, the origins of energy in the human reactive system, as well as certain drives and response tendencies, presumably possess instinctive bases.

Freud

Freud posits a theory of the origin of group formation. He discusses no principles of the dynamics of groups once they are formed, nor does he postulate a methodology to aid in the examination of group structure. Yet, Freud's limited writing on the matter was to influence greatly the substance and vocabulary of future systems of social psychology. He was so very concerned with the functioning of single human beings that his theoretical focus never strayed from that subject for long. Perhaps for this reason he is not in the mainstream of comprehensive theoretical concern about social behavior, as is Solomon Asch, for example. Nevertheless, one may notice that even Asch devotes an entire section of his *Social Psychology* to the role of the ego in social behavior. At the very minimum, Freud provides a beginning for a way of examining social behavior which others, such as Karen Horney, were to take up with great vigor and insight.

The substance of Freud's theory of social behavior, if we may call it that, is contained in his two monographs, *Group Psychology and the Analysis of the Ego,* and *The Ego and the Id,* first published in 1921, and 1923, respectively. Without attempting to summarize Freud's theory of the development of behavior, highly relevant but available in a number of other sources (e.g., Ruth Monroe, 1955), we shall discuss certain of his discoveries and summarize his theory of the emergence of social behavior, to arrive at the assumptions relevant to social activity.

Unlike behavioristic or gestalt theory, Freud's does not provide an easy translation from a particular philosophical system to the principles of the resulting theory itself. Although Freud certainly works from a bias regarding relevant empirical data, he is not experimental in even a loose sense of the term, nor is he concerned with the empirical demonstration that has been part of the gestalt approach. He is not clearly in either the Humean or the Kantian tradition regarding the nature of causality. In many ways, he represents a third great approach to modern psychological theory.

Even on the question of reducing explanations about social behavior to those concerning individual behavior, Freud's solution is unique. He is mainly concerned with the formation of groups—not with their dynamics once formed. He concludes that there is no essential division between individual and social psychology. "In the individual's mental life someone else is invariably involved, as a model, as an object, as a helper, as an opponent; and so from the very first individual psychology, in this extended but entirely justifiable sense of the words, is at the same time social psychology as well" (Freud, 1960, p. 3). Consequently, it is not really meaningful to ask whether the principles of social behavior are reducible to those of individual behavior. Both individual and social forms of activity are explained within a single set of terms involving, mainly, the ego and the id.

Since the energy source of all human activity stems from the biologically given libido, in which the sexual component is of central importance, and since another human being is necessary for complete sexual fulfillment, individual behavior is determined principally by relationships existing between at least two individuals. Social activity is derived from this sexual base. As family structure is the natural starting point of sexual relations, understanding the formation of a social group begins within that unit. No special instinct is needed to account for group behavior. The old one of eros is sufficient. Although Freud admits that there may be a separate explanation for the behavior of an individual in a crowd (in the sense of "mob"), social behavior in more cohesive social groups is motivated by the principles of individual behavior. Groups have both a primitive and a civilized aspect. When individuals come together in a group, their inhibitions may fall away and they may regress to the behavior of a child; all the cruel and destructive instincts which have been lying dormant become manifest. However, groups are also capable of high achievements in relation to an ideal. For example, they are capable of great sacrifices in the name of the ideal. This occurs under the influence of a leader. Freud's theory of the group centers around the process of suggestion by a group leader who represents an ego-ideal to the members of the group. Freud also develops an historical, or prototypic, theory of group formation which begins with the formation of the family.

"Libido" refers to those energies which have to do with the perpetuation of life through love, whether this be by direct sexual love, or by one of its derivatives, such as friendship, love of parents and children, love for humanity, etc. These love relationships constitute the essential dynamic of the group mind and the reasons for group existence as well. In groups with leaders (there are also leaderless groups), the leader is one who loves all members equally (as in the church and army, Freud's now classic examples). The leader's relation to the group is that of a kind elder brother (substitute father). Thus, there is quite obviously a similarity between group structure and the family. Since the illusion is preserved that all are loved equally by the leader, the members love one another in brotherly fashion. The individual is bound in two directions, to the leader and to the members of the group. The ties are of love and, hence, of deep emotion, and the individual lacks a great deal of personal freedom within the group situation. Conversely, groups without leaders, those based upon an ideal or abstraction, are not as primitive as led groups, and the members possess greater individual freedom of action.

Freud concentrates his analysis upon the led group, however, which he sees as more pervasive and historically older than the leaderless group. The essential dynamic aspect of a group is its love relationships existing between leader and member and between member and member. Yet, in almost every intense emotional situation existing between individuals, such as husband and wife, parent and child, friend and friend, there is a sediment of hostility and aversion which escapes detection only through repression. Freud attributes this hostility to a basic need for self-preservation on the part of an individual who exists in such emotional juxtaposition with another. Reactions to strangers are even more openly and intensely negative for the same reason. Within a group, however, negativity towards other members of the group vanishes so long as the group is intact. This is because of the existence of the member's libidinal ties with the leader and with other group members. These libidinal ties disrupt the self-defensive hostility of the individual, since primitive narcissism is weakened by the redirection of love outward to another.

Early in life a child begins to identify with the same-sexed parent and to take on some of his or her characteristic modes of response or appearance. This identification implies an emotional tie with the other person. Freud describes identification as the earliest expression of an emotional tie of one person to another. A small boy, for example, wishes to do what his father does, go where he goes, act the way he acts. He takes his father as an ideal whose behavior and attitudes are to be copied. At roughly the same time that this identification with the father appears, the boy develops a true object-cathexis toward his mother. He now exhibits two distinct ties: identification with the father, and a sexual object-cathexis toward the mother. In the child's natural development toward a unified mental life, the two ties eventually come together and the normal Oedipus complex comes about. Identification with the father takes on a hostile aspect and becomes identical with the desire to replace the father who is the mother's object of affection. This is also the basis of the ambivalent character of identification in the first place. It can result in tenderness or in the desire for removal of the individual toward whom the identification occurs.

Identification with the father, and the choice of the father as an object, can be distinguished. In the first case, the father is what the boy would like to be, and in the second, he has what the boy would like to have. Thus, the distinction depends upon whether the tie attaches to the subject or to the object of the ego. Identification is a process whereby a person's own ego is molded after the fashion of the one taken as a model. It is the original form of emotional tie with an object. It may develop when a person perceives a quality which he shares with another who is not an object of the sexual instinct. In summary, we may quote Freud regarding identification and group formation: "We already begin to divine that the mutual tie between members of a group is in the nature of an identification of this kind, based upon an important emotional common quality; and we may suspect that this common quality lies in the nature of the tie with the leader" (*Group Psychology,* p. 50).

The process of identification and other developments yield a split in the ego such that an "ego-ideal" is formed. The ego-ideal has the function of a "conscience," that is, of a repressor and censor to the ego. When a single individual, such as a leader, is taken in place of the ego-ideal by several individuals, who consequently identify with one another because of this substitution, a primary group has been formed. Freud analyzes the group in its primitive beginnings to conclude that group psychology, represented by the primal horde, actually predates individual psychology. The sons of a common father, prevented from satisfying their sexual instincts directly, caused the first group to emerge. There were emotional ties with the father who enforced sexual continence and, hence, emotional ties developed among the sons. The primal father became the group ideal, governing the group in place of the ego-ideal. Thus, the group depends upon ties which have originated from the inhibition of sexual instincts. It follows that the direct expression of sexual impulses is unfavorable to the formation of groups. Here we see an attempt to reduce explanation of the nature of social activity to explanation of the nature of sexual libido. However, the psychoanalytic methodology, requiring the confrontation of therapist with patient in a dyadic relation, may preclude the possibility that this reduction can ever be convincingly made.

Pervasiveness of Freud's Group Psychology

A strong similarity exists between the observations and thinking of Freud and those typically made by novelists, poets, and artists of different genres. All observe human beings actually living their daily lives. The units of observation include large portions of interrelated patterns of past history, simultaneously operating environmental stimulations, and capabilities and characteristics already present in the organism. Since he was well grounded in the biological sciences, it is not surprising that Freud placed the origins of human energy in the physiology of the organism, in a dynamic as well as a physical sense. He insisted that sexually based motivation was the principal font of behavior. But, aside from this, his way of observing the individual, especially in the group setting, retained the sense of drama and scope one expects from great literature.

Of particular relevance is his analysis of the primitive origins of group formation and the development of cooperation among men after the killing of the father in the primal horde. Freud compares the ancient state of affairs, where the father reigned sexually supreme, to the modern situation in which the father is individual family head. Even in ancient times, fathers were limited in their relations with one another, and formed a community of brothers. In seeking to re-establish the supremacy of an all-powerful father, the first epic poet, by sublimating his own impulses, attempted to resurrect the old powerful father figure, and created the heroic myth. The father and hero was he who had himself slain the father, thus preserving the memory of the original deed, but also preserving the idea that a community of brothers living in peace with one another was a necessity. The poet thus casts the ego-ideal in the form of the hero. It seems certain that Freud was giving an interpretation of the beginnings of Greek mythology where the primal act is the vanquishing of the Titan fathers by the sons who replace them as hero-father ideals. This myth, and all those that follow it, become the means by which the individual emerges from the primal group. Freud was either inspired by literature, especially the traditional Greek myths, to interpret mythology using his newly discovered personality theory, or he was actually inspired by the myths to form his personality theory. Since the psychoanalytic interview undoubtedly provided much of Freud's theoretical inspiration, it is most likely true that the process of influence occurred in both directions.

The validity of Freud's interpretation is open to investigation from a point of view different from the usual scientific one of utilizing empirical criteria. His theory is open to examination in terms of the rather inexplicable process which allows us to conclude that one novel or poem is better and more true about life than another. We can usually be convinced that a given novel is clearly better than another, and we are convinced that we can learn, profit from, or see some aspect of life more clearly from reading a good piece of fiction. The validity of Freud's interpretation is open to a similar kind of cognitive, common-sense, evaluative review. In some cases, he offends our credence and sensibilities. In others, we seem to understand a bit more for having read him. It is here that reduction of cognitive explanation to that based upon physiological drives seems impossible.

It is possible, of course, to judge Freud's theories in a completely empirical, scientific manner. We can establish checkable criteria for "cures" among patients diagnosed as mentally ill who have submitted to an intensive Freudian psychoanalytic treatment. There are many difficulties in establishing criteria for cure, to say the least, but the *form* of the evaluative procedure is available should we be able to supply the details. Within this context, Freud might have appreciated a functional-reductive analysis. However, we might again emphasize that the essentially non-scientific means of interpreting Freud is also available to us. In many ways, this look at human behavior is the kind a traditional gestalt psychologist might emphasize. It lacks, however, the discipline which the gestalter would most likely insist upon in structuring criteria of theoretical validity.

Psychologists sometimes are fond of paying lip service to the insights regarding human behavior supplied by the good novelist or poet, but these insights perhaps can never be included, even in form, in modern psychological systems. However, the insightful interpretation of human behavior may result in better predictions of important human events than those that can be gleaned from many empirical systems. A man, having read Dostoyevsky's *Notes From The Underground,* for example, may better predict whether a given individual will commit suicide, compared with the man basing his prediction upon a psychological system such as Skinner's, Lewin's, or Freud's. This indicates that even the systems of Lewin and Freud may, to an extent, be fractionated in that they do not include the possibility of understanding many complex forms of human activity.

Conclusions

It is apparent that for Freud, social behavior is a product of the instinctually based motivational system of the organism. That is, because social activity evolves from certain relations, especially those existing between the id and the ego which involve the ego-ideal, its explanation is similar to that of the functioning of the id and the ego in the individual. In these systems, the energy for life is provided by the instincts of life and death (eros and thanatos). Thus, the need for entering into social activity is explained by a mechanism which operates initially at the biological level, and which involves sexual activity. Although Freud never stated so, one might safely predict that he would explain the complications of social activity which one observes in daily life in terms of the ego-ideal, which, in turn, is derivative from certain motivations instinctively based, though not necessarily in a physiological sense. For the individual, psychoanalysis becomes the rooting out of the pattern of influences in his life history which reflect the force of this original instinctual motivation. Here, we are again confronted with the difficulty of deciding to what degree Freud's interpretation of social activity is reductive.

Karen Horney

If it can be empirically supported that the best explanation regarding social activity need not be based upon the presupposition of the existence of a dominate libidinous energy system especially associated with a sexual component, then the nature of social activity can be placed upon an entirely different basis. The lack of strong empirical support for sexual emphasis within the framework of psychoanalytic therapy, and the possibility of other sources of important human motivation, prompted Karen Horney (1937, 1939) to diverge from Freud on this important theoretical issue. While following the methodological, therapeutic, and theoretical leads supplied by Freud, Horney shifted the emphasis regarding original sources of energy from instinctual ones to those born of the social nature of the organism. She developed a system which is, by conception, not reducible to the terms of a higher-level theory.

Horney, like Freud, did not develop a theory of social activity. She suggests no special methodology to examine the problem of group organization and dynamics. However, she does introduce the idea that, rather than being the result of instinctual human activities rooted in biology, society is the supplier of some of the major motivational patterns in modern Western man. The shift to a particular cultural milieu as the prime originator of patterns of behavior brings a tremendous pre-eminence to the data of cultural anthropology and sociology. They become highly relevant factors to the understanding of group and individual behavior within the psychoanalytic framework. Freud, we remember, was largely unconcerned with cultural factors within the theoretical structure of his theory.

While Freud's theory of personality is concerned with normal and neurotic individuals in all societies and for all time, Horney limits herself to the neurotic Westerner in the twentieth century. She rejects the notion that neuroses are to be understood totally through occurrences in the childhood of the individual. Unconscious tendencies in adulthood, which are not necessarily repetitions of childhood responses, are of equal importance. Modern neuroses are characterized by the individual's excessive dependency on the approval and affection of others. Only occasionally are sexual impulses found to be the dynamic force behind the formation of anxiety. Rather, hostile impulses form the main source of neurotic anxiety.

If there is a childhood history of a lack of genuine warmth and affection, feelings of being lonely and helpless in a hostile world pervade the existence of the individual. This gives rise to what Horney calls "basic anxiety," accompanied by a "basic hostility," which underlies the relationships of people both normal and neurotic. However, since the same cultural pressures and conflicts exist in both types of people, Horney considers basic anxiety to be an essentially neurotic manifestation. Western society is so constructed that there exists the need for competition in practically every phase of life. Individuals must fight with one another, and the success of one often implies the failure of another. This competitiveness gives rise to hostility in many aspects of daily living. As Freud recognized, it also exists within the family, between father and son, mother and daughter, etc. In a normal individual, where affection and warmth have prevailed in childhood, the basic anxiety is not usually accompanied by a great degree of hostility, as it is in the neurotic.

The competitiveness of modern Western society makes the individual feel isolated in a hostile world. He turns to the seeking and giving of affection to remedy the situation. It is for this reason that love (need for approval, affection, etc.) is overvalued in our society (especially in the United States) where competitiveness is intense and pervasive. Accepted social virtues are patent contradictions and help to create the atmosphere underlying neurotic conflict. The need to succeed and compete is emphasized alongside of the need to be humble, to love one's brother, and to be self-sacrificing. Furthermore, society stimulates our needs for social advancement and material possession in the face of the factual impossibility of satisfying them for most people.

It should be apparent that Horney, unlike Freud, does not believe it is possible to reduce explanation of human social activity to physiological principles. Her orientation is sociological and cultural, rather than psychological. Although it is difficult to speak of observational units within the framework of any psychoanalytically oriented theory, we may conclude that the emotional drive or force, as a total functioning entity, is the fundamental unit of her explanatory system. However, even with this major shift in emphasis, involving change in the unit of analysis and the possibility of reduction of some concepts, Horney's orientation remains similar to Freud's. Neither presents a theory of group activity or dynamics, or a methodology for examining the nature of social groups. Both Freud's system and Horney's extensive theoretical modification of it are approaches concerning the study of individual behavior, although other people enter as key objects in determining responses.

The psychoanalytic systems have largely provided specific "leads" to social psychological theorists, rather than providing a total theoretical context from which to build an explanation of the behavior of groups. Ideas such as the necessity to defend one's ego structure in the face of hostile or presumed hostile elements in the environment have entered into much psychological research and theory construction. The concept of striving for a tension equilibrium, although derivable from other theoretical sources as well, is a psychoanalytic emphasis which has been used extensively to interpret social behavior. However, the emphasis on empirical data gathered only from the psychoanalytic interview cancels the possibility of experimentation on actual group functioning, at least for the analyst who finds himself committed to examining the single individual as a necessary prerequisite for gaining insights into human behavior. Hence, the very method of obtaining empirical data within the framework of psycho-analytic theory makes it impossible to develop a psychoanalytic social theory which is empirically based. Either the system of explanation is closed, as in Freud's interpretation of social activity in terms of the instinctual foundations of behavior, or it can only suggest and hypothesize as to what the structure of a complete theory of social behavior based upon accumulation of empirical evidence might be.

Lorenz and Instinct

As we have seen, Freud's explanation of human social behavior begins with an emphasis upon certain biologically given, that is, instinctive, reaction tendencies in the organism. Although he focuses upon interactive patterns among family members to gather information about social activity, Freud's theory of social behavior is based upon the instinctive reaction tendencies. These are the energy sources of the organism. While Konrad Lorenz's (1963) ideas are far from being psychoanalytic in any sense of the term, he has emphasized the instinctive origins of certain forms of social behavior. He began with a thesis regarding instincts which is at least partially in opposition to the "death wish" occasionally invoked by Freud to explain aggressive behavior in man. Studying the natural behavior of animals, Lorenz concluded that aggressive behavior is clearly an instinct like any other, which in natural conditions functions to insure the survival of the individual and the species. Since aggressive behavior requires at least one other organism, either of the same or of a different species, it is fundamentally a social activity and can be studied as such. It will be fruitful to pursue Lorenz's reasons for assigning a large part of social aggressive behavior to instinctive determiners.

Lorenz begins by noticing that aggression among animals takes place almost exclusively among members of the same species. Even though animals who prey on other species for food are apparently engaged in interspecific aggression, they do so only to secure food, and cease when they are not hungry. Furthermore, the body posturing associated with intraspecific aggression is usually absent in interspecific aggression. From his laboratory and naturalistic observations, for example, Lorenz concludes that fish in general are much more aggressive towards members of their own species than towards members of others. Thus, the problem becomes to examine the reasons for aggression among like-species members, and to determine the function of this aggression in the life history of the single organism and the species. An easily observable function of aggressive behavior among members of the same species occurs when animals attack each other over a portion of territory. Territorial defense functions to control the numbers of animals in any given area and, thus, to conserve the available food supply. The survival value of aggression in this situation is obvious. Two other major survival values of aggression are selection of the strongest by rival fights, and the protection of the young. The process of aggression against members of the same species is more complicated, however, than is apparent from a simple listing of the various survival functions it serves. Within groups of animals living together in a limited space, especially when confined in a specific area such as a cage, a "pecking order" quite frequently develops. This is a hierarchy based on the relative strength of the animals, and on the resulting possibilities for aggression. The function of the pecking order seems to be to reduce total aggression, in that animals generally will not attack others higher in the hierarchy. The limited fighting which results seems to serve the purpose of teaching the young of the horde how to fight and in some cases, for example, the jackdaws, how to recognize a predatory enemy. Lorenz believes that an aggressive drive builds up in the organism regardless of the external stimulus conditions present, and that it must be discharged, in most cases, against another member of the species. Male East Indian cichlids will attack and destroy their mates if a "scapegoat" fish, a male of the same species, is not present in the tank to allow a release of aggression. Men on polar expeditions living in closely knit groups have their aggressive drives dammed up by their friendliness towards and dependence upon other members of the group. This, coupled with the absence of outsiders on which they may vent their aggression, leads to more frequent disruptive blowups within the group than if the men were working and living under normal conditions.

Over Evolutionary Time

Aggressive behavior often is refined so that, although the aggressive tendency remains, the attack is redirected to render it harmless to some members of the same species. These redirected attacks become ritualized patterns of behavior in many animals and in man. Examples of these ritualized "ceremonies" can be seen in cichlids and geese. While mating, the female cichlid, at first submissive, becomes extremely aggressive, placing herself in the middle of the male's territorial waters and striking a pose consisting of the principal stimulus pattern which incites male cichlids to attack. The male, accordingly, charges the female. Just before ramming her, he veers off to one side leaving the female unharmed, and furiously attacks another member of his species, usually his territorial neighbor. Thus, the attack activity is released by one stimulus and discharged at another. The first stimulus (the female cichlid in aggressive pose) is stimulus both for the male's aggression and for the inhibition of its discharge. In the animal kingdom, redirected aggressive activity often takes the form of ritualistic behavior which apparently serves the function of releasing aggression in a manner harmless to the preservation of the species. In the fight between male rivals of many species, fallow deer or wolves, for example, the selection of the stronger is accomplished without the destruction of the weaker male. Fighting between male fallow deer takes place largely through the locking of antlers and concomitant pushing and pulling. Should one of the combatants pull away and retreat, thus exposing an unprotected part of his body, the other animal stops his charge until both animals are in a head to head position or the fight is clearly over and one has been established as the winner. Thus, the rival represents both the stimuli to begin and to inhibit aggression, depending upon body position and behavior. A similar type of ritual occurs among male wolves.

Lorenz makes an analogy between this phylogenetic ritualized behavior in animals and the cultural origin of symbols in human society. He visualizes the celebrated smoking of the peace-pipe among North American Indians as an aggression inhibiting ritual similar in function to that of animals. The smile upon greeting might also have this function. In both animals and human beings, these rituals, having at one time served a direct purpose, may persist through habit even though they have lost their original meaning. Both animals and men prefer making the same movements in, and expecting the same results from, their environment during most of their waking hours. Lorenz remarks that human social behavior is so permeated by cultural ritualization that most of us are unaware of its presence. Even at their most unrefined level, "good manners" are required by any society, and if someone does not conform to these expectations, his behavior is taken to be equivalent to an act of overt hostility. Hence, "good manners" function as appeasement rituals signifying the inhibition of aggressive behavior.

Lorenz's conclusion, and perhaps his major point, is that human social behavior is determined not only by cultural tradition and learning, but also by the laws of phylogenetically adapted instinctive behavior. Over evolutionary time, those animals, such as the raven or wolf, who are physically endowed with the equipment to kill other animals of their own size, have developed inhibitions preventing them from injuring or killing members of their own species under natural conditions. In animals such as the dove or man where there is rarely the possibility of their injuring or killing one another with a single peck, bite or blow, inhibitions against injuring members of the same species have not developed. Under unnatural conditions where animals of this type are cornered or are living in captivity, they can kill one another in a slow, painful manner without any inhibitions arising. As Lorenz has said,

One can only deplore the fact that man has definitely not got a carnivorous mentality! All his trouble arises from his being a basically harmless, omnivorous creature, lacking in natural weapons with which to kill big prey, and, therefore, also devoid of the built-in safety devices which prevent "professional" carnivores from abusing their killing power to destroy fellow members of their own species (1963, p. 241).

Man has moved ahead of his physical evolution, in the negative sense, for there has been little time to develop killing instincts which are now necessary because, in inventing artificial weapons, man thus has upset the equilibrium of killing potential and socially relevant inhibitions. It is as if by some unnatural trick of nature, the dove "has suddenly acquired the beak of a raven" (Lorenz, 1963, p. 241).

Ultimately, then, human social norms, rites, and symbols are phylogenetically evolved behavior patterns, the adherence to which, over time, becomes habitual in the individual member of the group. The fundamental character of social norms is instinctive and rooted in aggression and its control. Lorenz states that "Humanity is not enthusiastically combative because it is split into political parties, but it is divided into opposing camps because this is the adequate stimulus situation to arouse militant enthusiasm in a satisfying manner" (1963, p. 271).

To the extent that social behavior is instinctive, attempts to study that aspect of it will need to concentrate upon the physiology of the organism, and upon the organism's behavioral history over evolutionary time. Reduction of explanation of some social activity to the terms of physiological and behavioral explanation will be possible. Response manipulation in the manner of the functionalists is irrelevant, except as a method for exploring the limits of instinctively given behavior patterns. The holistic theorists' concentration upon total patterns of behavior, and upon the isomorphism presumably existing between these patterns and those of central nerve physiology, might possibly incorporate, with less damage to their position, the idea that much social behavior has an instinctive origin. In any case, to the extent that Lorenz's position is correct, a new and significant dimension is added to the study of social behavior in modern times, a dimension to which William MacDougall was sensitive in 1908, when he wrote what became one of the first American textbooks of social psychology.

Summary Chart of the Status of Principal Psychoanalytic Theories on Assumptive Characteristics Relevant to Social Activity

ASSUMPTION	THEORY	
	Freud	*Horney*
REDUCTION OF PRINCIPAL CONCEPTS	Yes—By way of explanation of physiological characteristics of organism	Yes—By way of explanation of individual experience
	No—In that fundamental character of man only totally understandable in the social context	No—Explanation of social activity not reducible to explanation based on physiological concepts
CAUSALITY	Productive (necessity involved) Tradition—Kant and Hume?	Productive (necessity involved) Tradition—Kant and Hume?
GENERAL METHODOLOGY	Explanation through dyadic interaction unit of patient and therapist	Explanation through dyadic interaction unit of patient and therapist
USE OF STATISTICS	None	None
RESEARCH TIME PERSPECTIVE	Historical (great emphasis)	Historical (great emphasis)

chapter

7

The Theory of
Cognitive Dissonance

The theory of social behavior which most successfully has captured the imagination of researchers and theorists in the past decade is that advocated by Leon Festinger in *A Theory of Cognitive Dissonance* (1957). Festinger's theory attempts to predict what people will do and how they will think under various conditions which exist in their cognitive life. The unit of the system is the cognition, which may be loosely defined as a thought which is verbally expressable by the individual. This might be, among others, an opinion, attitude, or belief. Should one object to the looseness of the concept of cognition, and thus question its appropriateness as the unit of Festinger's system, it need only be pointed out that its various manifestations are found in rather specific, empirical contexts in the course of the development of the theory. For example, in a study of advertisement reading preferences of new car owners, the dependent variable and, hence, the cognition predicted from dissonance theory, was a preference for viewing and reading certain automobile advertisements rather than others.

We shall not attempt to examine the tremendous amount of empirical work which has been inspired by this theory, or the criticisms which have been made of it. Its validity along empirical dimensions is of but peripheral concern to us. We shall be interested rather in its form as a system of explanation, and in its inherent possi-bilities and limitations as a theory of social activity.

Festinger's cognitive dissonance represents an interesting cross between the functional-reductive and the conceptual type of theories. Since there is no suggestion that the fundamental unit of the system, the cognition, is reducible to the terms of a different level system (for example, to those of physiology), and since the unit is con-sidered to be unique to human beings (or, at least, to higher animals), we may conclude, in short, that the theory is firmly non-reductive in outlook. It focuses upon an important, sometimes indirectly ob-servable, total bit of human activity which is complete in itself. It thus marks the point at which explanation must begin.

In this sense, the theory is more similar to those we have dis-cussed under the holistic label than to those of a functional or psy-choanalytic type. However, the principal dynamic of the system is that of "drive toward equilibrium," which is more typical of biologically oriented, "reductive" behavior theories of the kind discussed in Chapter Four. In other words, a non-cognitive mechanical principle is used to explain changes in a particular kind of cognitive function-ing. Perhaps one of the reasons the theory became popular so rapidly is just this aspect of combining biological mechanistic dynamics with a non-reducible, "meaningful" (as discussed in Chapter Five) unit of explanation.

For American psychologists, the heritage of gestalt psychology is strong, although not as strong as that stemming from early be-haviorism. A theory which combines aspects of both positions is understandably satisfying. It also represents, in a minor way, an integration of the two great modes of thinking, the Humean and the Kantian. The general principles of the theory must be dealt with in some detail to examine the form of explanation it represents, as well as its potential and actual success in explaining various facets of human social activity.

Festinger initially assumes that individuals enjoy and strive for consistency (consonance) in their personal and social behavior. If an individual believes in heavy government involvement in social wel-fare, for example, he most likely believes that medicare is a good policy. He is also likely to act in a manner which he believes to be consistent with his beliefs (for example, to vote for a liberal as opposed to conservative candidate for president). On many occasions the individual finds inconsistencies (dissonance) in his life. He is addicted to sweets, but knows he has a weight problem which is bad for his health. If he cannot immediately remove this inconsistency (for example, by eliminating sweets), he is likely to feel at least periodically uncomfortable with this dissonance. The principal tenet of Festinger's system is that this dissonance will create a state of drive or energy to think or act so as to attempt to reduce or remove the dissonance and achieve consonance. The dissonance exists in his cognitions, which are consciously, that is, verbally, available to him at almost any time.

The individual will attempt to reduce or eliminate completely the cognitive dissonance which has arisen in a given situation. There are a number of ways in which he does this. (In fact, most of Festinger's treatment deals with attempts at reducing or eliminating dissonance.) When dissonance is present, the individual will also actively avoid situations which would be likely to increase it.

Dissonance arises in the life of the individual because "new events may happen or new information may become known to a person, creating at least a momentary dissonance with existing knowledge, opinion, or cognition concerning behavior" (Festinger, 1957, p. 4). It arises in the daily living situation of the individual. As Festinger remarks, "very few things are all black or all white; very few situations are clear cut enough so that opinions or behaviors are not to some extent a mixture of contradictions" (1957, p. 5). In order to reduce dissonance the individual might change his cognitions by changing his behavior, or he might change his "knowledge" about the cognition involved. That is, he may seek new information, or distort the old, so as to render the idea which has determined the dissonance untenable. For example, if one is confronted with information that cigarette smoking is harmful to one's health and one enjoys smoking, a dissonance arises. It is possible to eliminate the dissonance by ceasing to smoke, or to reduce the dissonance by concluding that the evidence is flimsy regarding the deleterious effects of smoking.

It perhaps will be useful to illustrate both the meaning of cognitive dissonance and its ease of application to social psychological situations by attempting to work out its implications for a problem to which it has not been systematically applied. In recent years there has been a good bit of interest in opinion and attitude change as a function of the order of presentation of two opposed persuasive arguments. Is the first argument or the second more influential in changing the subject's opinion in the direction advocated by that argument? If the first argument is more successful in changing opinion in its direction, a "primacy effect" is said to occur. If the second argument is more successful, a "recency effect" is said to occur.

In order to predict an order effect from the theory of cognitive dissonance, it is necessary to determine the initial (pre-experimental) opinion of the subject, whether negative, positive, or neutral. This may be done through the administration of a questionnaire. If the individual is neutral with respect to the point of view, then no prediction of order effects is possible from the cognitive dissonance position. If the initial opinion is positive, however, and the succeeding opposed communications are administered in "con-pro" and "pro-con" orders to different groups of subjects, then a nonsignificant order effect would be predicted for the following reasons. The group receiving the "con" communication first would perceive dissonance between its negative content and the group's own positive stand on the issue. When the "pro" communication is presented shortly afterward, a solution to the felt dissonance is possible if the subjects move further toward the "pro" point of view. Thus, a recency effect results. The counterbalance group, receiving the communication in the "pro-con" order, perceives no dissonance at the time of the "pro" communication, but does perceive dissonance when the "con" presentation is made. This group responds by moving toward the "pro" communication and, hence, a primacy effect occurs. The groups, counterbalanced for order of presentation of the communications, are analyzed together; their opposing response tendencies cancel one another, and no order effect results.

A recency effect predicted from the cognitive dissonance position would occur when the initial opinion (positive or negative) is different from the first presented argument (either "pro" or "con"), and the dissonance resolution is made by moving toward the second argument. When initial opinion is the same as the first presented argument, then a primacy effect is predicted. If the initial opinion of one of the two groups is similar to the second presented argument, then a nonsignificant order effect is predicted. The discussion is summarized in Table 1.

If the empirical results of order-effect research (e.g., Lana, 1961, 1963a, 1963b, 1964; Rosnow and Russell, 1963; Thomas, Webb, and Tweedie, 1961; Schultz, 1963) are examined, it will be obvious that only about half of the above predictions actually have occurred. However, the reader should be reminded that these predictions were made by the present writer from what he believed to be the necessary derivatives of dissonance theory regarding the order-effect problem, and were not made by Dr. Festinger.

Festinger points out that his theory is in the form of a general idea, such that other concepts, "hunger" or "frustration," for example, could be substituted for "dissonance" with the hypotheses retaining the same form and being equally meaningful. The biological notion of homeostasis or internal bodily equilibrium is the historical precedent whose form Festinger has borrowed. Freud and Hull, to mention only two theorists, had previously utilized the concept of "drive toward equilibrium" as one of the major dynamic devices in their systems. Both, however, kept such a dynamic well anchored in the physiological processes. For Freud, the sexual part of the libido provided the dynamic source of energy and, hence, of cyclical equilibrium and disequilibrium; while, for Hull, it was provided by the cyclical bodily processes (hunger, thirst, sex, motor activity, etc.). There is no such anchoring with Festinger. The validity of his system must come from evidence which is independent of physiology. Discounting the extensive criticism (e.g., Chapanis and Chapanis, 1964) which has been made concerning the support of

Table 1 Interpretation of Cognitive Dissonance Predictions for Order Effects in Persuasive Communications

INITIAL OPINION	* Positive	Negative	N P	N N	P P
ORDER OF ARGUMENTS	*Pro* / Con	*Con* / Pro	P C / *C* P	*C* P / P *C*	C *P* / *P* C
ORDER EFFECT	Primacy (no dissonance both groups)		Recency (dissonance both groups)	No effect (dissonance one group)	No effect (dissonance one group)

Underlined argument is predicted to have the greatest influence on the subject in determining opinion change according to its dissonance-resolving potential.

* Each positive and negative pair represents two comparable groups of subjects.

the theory via empirical evidence, we find that Festinger makes what may be a *salto mortale* from the physiological notion of homeostasis to the "drive to reduce cognitive dissonance." As mentioned above, by Festinger's own admission, "hunger" or "frustration" could be substituted for "dissonance." Thus, along a very important dimension he equates a distinctly cognitive process with processes which have a definite physiological basis (e.g., those involved in hunger), as well as those which are probably both physiological and behavioral (e.g., those involved in frustration). Yet there is no direct reference to the possibility of the reduction of cognitive dissonance to physiological deprivation and to the increase in energy which usually accompanies deprivation. There is no question, however, that Festinger uses the idea of equilibrium, as it is usually used in a physiological context, as a process which is of great importance in understanding opinions and attitudes in the social situation. We find that the system implies a kind of reduction, at least in the *form* of explanation used at the cognitive level to the form of a possible explanation at the physiological level. The validity of the homeostatic "cognitive" assumption depends totally upon its empirical validity; that is, its ability to predict changes in opinion, attitude, belief, or behavior. There is no contradiction in the idea that cognitive processes may have a dynamic characteristic similar to bodily physiological ones, and yet not be reducible to them. Actually, the position is consistent with the monism rigorously reintroduced into modern science in the late 19th century (see Mach, in Chapter Three above) and which continues to the present day. Usually, however, there is an accompanying, but not logically necessary, supplemental assumption that cognitive terms eventually will be reduced to those of physiology.

Because many modern theorists see a huge empirical, if not logical, gap between explaining cognitive and explaining physiological processes by the same theory, Festinger's jump might seem facile and unconvincing. It is also simplistic, which mitigates its being first perceived as a possible explanation for such apparently complex behavior as attitudes, beliefs and opinions.

Festinger makes no attempt to trace or explain the nature of the "drive for cognitive consonance" which, he postulates, exists in human beings. In the case of physiologically based drives, tissue need, central nervous system changes, and local conditions are often assumed to be the factors which yield increased energy level (drive) in the organism. Festinger does not attempt this type of analysis. He simply assumes that cognitive dissonance gives rise to a drive state, and develops his theory from this point. Further validation from this stage would require empirical support. The question of the validity of Festinger's system as it stands reduces to whether or not predictions of behavioral and/or cognitive changes in the organism can be successfully made, the answer to which is beyond the scope of this book. Instead, we shall look at the principal hypotheses of the system, to see what they mean in terms of a total, behaving human being, and what they mean as abstract concepts within a system which can possibly predict aspects of human behavior, for example, opinion change.

If I say that a man will seek to change his opinion about the fattening power of sweets, or stop eating sweets, or forget about the entire problem, or recognize the negative characteristics of eating sweets but counterbalance this with positive characteristics (e.g., the body needs sugar), or if the man uses some other means to remove or reduce the drive which presumably has arisen because of the felt cognitive inconsistency, he is acting either logically (giving up the sweets or being genuinely convinced they would be more harmful in the breach than in the consumption, etc.) or illogically (repressing the entire problem, rationalizing, etc.). By "logically," we mean simply that he acts consistently with his self-defined desires. In both instances, he may succeed in reducing a drive state by eliminating the cognitive dissonance. Thus, within the framework of dissonance theory, the process of a man thinking in a logically consistent manner (e.g., I do not wish to gain weight; I eat a lot of sweets, sweets produce weight, therefore, I shall either have to give up sweets or forget about being slim.) has the same status for reducing dissonance as the man who handles the elimination of drive due to dissonance in an illogical manner (e.g., I believe it is not the sweets I eat that produce the weight, but my glandular system which operates independently of anything I may eat, etc.). Both approaches, and many others as well, will eliminate the drive arising from cognitive dissonance, but they are of markedly different varieties. The theory of cognitive dissonance lumps these various types of responses together, glossing over their differences, because they presumably share a capacity to eliminate dissonance. If indeed they do possess this capacity, there is no error in lumping them together for purposes of prediction. However, this implicitly assumes that opinion, attitude change, and other types of social behavior have a rather similar structure and dynamic, an assumption which one would be hard pressed to defend. The change in an individual's opinion about the Democratic party because of a change in its platform, for example, does not represent the same psychological or social situation as in the case of a man who changes his opinion because he has found out that the party has appointed Negroes to key positions within it. Even if both opinion change situations fit within the predictions derivable from cognitive dissonance theory, much of the meaningful aspects of the situation are passed over.

We must conclude that, although the system uses for its unit of analysis cognitions which are direct expressions of the complexity of the social context, its dependence upon the homeostatic-type equilibrium concept has nullified much of this unit's potential. This is a criticism of what the system does not do, however. In all fairness, it must be emphasized that Festinger's claims are restricted to predicting various changes in cognition and behavior. Whether the system predicts what is claimed for it is an empirical question. We are simply suggesting its inherent limitations, which it shares with Skinner's and other functionally oriented systems. On the other hand, because Festinger has begun his system of social behavior with a "meaningful" unit of analysis, the system may be useful within these limits.

Summary Chart of the Status of Cognitive Dissonance Theory on Assumptive Characteristics Relevant to Social Activity

ASSUMPTION	THEORY
	Festinger Cognitive Dissonance
REDUCTION OF PRINCIPAL CONCEPTS	Yes—In form of explanation No—No reference to other than social phenomena
CAUSALITY	Functional—contingency Productive—not opposed Tradition—Hume and Kant?
GENERAL METHODOLOGY	Explanation through experimentation and prediction of, clearly defined responses—but a generally mixed functional-reductive and holistic methodology
USE OF STATISTICS	Moderate No conceptual opposition
RESEARCH TIME PER-SPECTIVE	Ahistorical by emphasis rather than by conception Historical in certain situations

part III

Methodology and Prospectus

Another shift in perspective is necessary in these last two chapters. Chapter Eight deals in greater detail with the methodological differences of the various theories discussed in Chapters Four through Seven, and concentrates on the methodology of the functional-reductive and holistic theories. Since psychoanalysis and cognitive dissonance fall more or less within their purview, less attention is paid to the unique aspects of their methodologies than to characteristics derivable from the Humean and Kantian positions on cause and effect and to the reductive positions which follow from them. Attention also is given to the statistical methodology which permeates these approaches, in order to see more clearly the explanatory possibilities of the various theory categories. Chapter Eight concludes with a brief account of the mathematics involved in the construction of mathematical models used to explain certain types of social activity. Differences and similarities between the use of mathematics in constructing models and in evaluating data are also discussed.

Chapter Nine provides some general summary and stresses those areas in social psychology that need reconceptualization. Possibilities and limitations of current systems are discussed within the context of empirical problems. These are extensions of the theoretical issues examined earlier in the book. Creativity and the nature of the creative genius are discussed within the context of the functional-reductive theories. Creativity is seen to be an example of complex human behavior that may require a markedly different approach from those previously used to deal with it.

The two final sections of Chapter Nine suggest other avenues of solution to some problems associated with complex areas of human social existence which have been either avoided or handled inadequately by the theories reviewed. Explanation of social phenomena by literary exposition is briefly explored, and it is suggested that this kind of methodological approach may follow from the *a priori* focus discussed earlier. There is also a section on Marshall McLuhan's attempt to explain communication media and the effects of technology on behavior, emotion and cognition. McLuhan was chosen because he represents a fusion of a literary approach with an empirical technique that may be useful for the study of many aspects of social activity. The chapter concludes with the author's suggestions concerning possible directions in understanding certain problems arising from complex social activity. I have taken full advantage of what is usually the author's prerogative to be somewhat speculative in his final summary and perspective chapter. I am certain this will be extremely obvious to the reader.

chapter

8

Methodology

The preceding chapters were concerned primarily with the prevailing assumptions used to explain social activity. Since all of the theories discussed are empirically based, the way in which the data are gathered is of great importance for understanding the implications of the various assumptions. The assumptions of any system may lead, logically or empirically, to many choices of procedure. The theorist's actual choice is significant, for he may not have chosen the best method for supporting his particular contentions. A theorist's choice of methodology when he is developing the initial principles of his system involves the rejection of other, perhaps more useful, methodologies. Furthermore, the use of a particular method of gathering empirical evidence may make it impossible for the evidence to support a certain aspect of the theory.

Theory and empirically based methodology are linked, for a theory must have empirical referents which form the core of the psychological system. The choice of methodology, however, is limited by the choice of the often subtle initial principles of the system. Theorists usually understand this very well and proceed accordingly, but not always. For example, is it possible to predict creative behavior (however defined) by studying the functional contingencies between certain observable aspects of behavior and environmental variables which are directly or indirectly manipulated by the experimenter? Perhaps what we mean by "creative behavior" may preclude the

125

manipulation of the individual's environment in order to produce the behavior. To take another example, to insist that all "meaningful" social behavior must be studied *in toto* and *in situ* may disallow the possibility that a researcher may discover that a good part of this behavior involves a simpler process, for example, fear conditioning.

Although logical and empirical limitations are placed upon theory by the form of a particular methodology, methodological limitations placed upon theory by its form and content are found more frequently. Usually a theoretical structure is developed on the basis of the theorist's past experience with the subject matter. He eventually chooses a method of procedure which seems to make sense within the context of his tentative theoretical tenets. There is a somewhat compelling and perhaps logical aspect to this order. Yet, it is also true that theorists have embraced a particular methodology as being relevant for obtaining information about a given subject matter before they possessed any particular theory to explain it. In this case, one might argue that a tacit set of theoretical assumptions regarding the subject matter had been made by the individual choosing the "theory free" (for the time being) methodology. It seems that traditional American behaviorism followed this pattern, as well as, perhaps, behaviorism's modern offshoots.

There is no reason, of course, why a theorist should not begin his study with a methodology instead of with a set of theoretical assumptions. From whatever point the theorist chooses to proceed, however, there are first principles regarding the nature of the subject matter which must eventually be articulated to comprehend fully the theoretical system and the manner of evaluating its truth, limitations, and possibilities.

Within the context of social psychology, concerned as it is with individuals interacting with other individuals, the problem of a successful methodology is particularly acute. Perhaps the very first problem is that one is never quite sure what he should be studying. Although a similar problem exists in physiological or learning psychology, for example, the evolutionary assumption that one problem is meaningfully connected with another is useful for those areas. Thus, conditioning may be studied before one studies problem solving or abstract reasoning. Within the traditional areas of social psychology, all problems seem to be equally complex. As we have seen in previous chapters, part of the modern solution has been a necessary fractionation into manageable problem units, with the hope that the task of reconstructing the whole will not be as difficult as it was for all the king's men. Should one be satisfied with a choice of subject matter within the context of social activity, the next problem is how to define and measure units relevant to the test of an hypothesis which either has been derived from theory or is temporarily theory free. Theorists who start from different assumptive bases handle the problem in different ways.

The Functionalists

It is perhaps apparent that the prediction of various types of conditioned responses involving relatively simple reactions on the part of an organism may be made by studying functional relations existing between identifiable environmental conditions and simple responses. It is not so apparent that the same study will be successful in predicting social activity. If we examine the general procedure of Skinner or Skinnerians (e.g., Sidman, 1960) we see that its most important goal is to establish, through manipulations made by the experimenter, the conditions impinging upon the organism at the time a relevant dependent variable (in the form of some observable behavior) is being measured. For example, one must establish the normal rate of response of an animal to a given environmental situation (such as pressing a bar, or entering a passage), while ascertaining the previous length of time the animal has been deprived of food, water, etc. In short, it is necessary to establish the "steady state behavior" of the organism before an experiment designed to gather new information about a response can be tested. Sidman (1960) defines "steady state behavior" as behavior the characteristics of which do not change over long periods of time. Some criterion must be used, of course, to decide when a steady state has been reached in the organism's performance.

Since most functional theorists have been interested mainly in simple learning phenomena, the discovery of the relevant steady state of the organism has been a somewhat simple task. But, how does one establish a steady state with respect to those environmental conditions and response patterns usually associated with social activity? Perhaps it is possible to do so, but there are great difficulties. It seems that it is never possible to utilize directly an experimental technique which allows all or most of the relevant independent variables to be manipulated by the experimenter in order to produce a steady state when the behavior in question is what we ordinarily think of as social. What we mean by social behavior or activity is necessarily a product of past conceptual behavior and of behavior which involves the direct or indirect intervention of other persons. One would have to synchronize the pretest conditions both of the subject and of the individuals who were to play a major independent (in the technical sense) role in predicting his behavior. It is true, however, that were a Skinnerian to accept this argument, he might fall back on the behavioral analysis of language to explain social behavior in a functional manner. There has been no major experimental attempt to support Skinner's system of verbal behavior, however, and the necessary methodology remains something for the future.

Skinner's functional methodology, based as it is upon discovering a relevant steady state in the organism, is insufficient to deal with social behavior as an observable phenomenon *after* it has been established in the organism. The idea of the steady state is used to reproduce the conditions which might *naturally* have occurred in the history of the organism and which might be relevant to the particular phenomenon under study. Skinner's methodology is a way of studying the formation of social activity, rather than of examining its nature once it is complete. Consequently, we may identify the major portion of the functional approach to be an examination of phenomena "before the fact."

Many other methodologies, as we shall see, depend, at least in part, on *ex post facto* analyses. However, the functional approach depends upon a developmental as opposed to an *ex post facto* methodology, and utilizes environmental and response contingencies to yield predictions, which indicates that it must fall back on *ex post facto* analysis when explaining already formed social behavior. Skinner (1948) does this in his novel, *Walden II*. The method is always historical in the face of already existing behavior. Its great, and perhaps only, strength lies in its ability to shape behavior into whatever form is desired. We may conclude, as have others, that Skinner's system is mainly a way of examining animal and human behavior; that is, it is mainly a methodology. The means of changing or shaping society are at the same time the means for understanding it. For better or worse, this is the principal legacy for social psychology of the functional-reductive position. And Skinner's system is the most coherent, consistent and ingenious within this framework.

Having drawn the above conclusion, it is important to look further at several of the technical features of Skinner's functional methodology. Steady states and control of relevant variables may be established in a given experiment, but most scientists are not satisfied with the results of a single undertaking. The principal reason for this is that many unknown factors might have been operating to yield a particular result. If this is acknowledged, the next problem becomes how to handle the repetition of an experiment so that the probability of occurrence of the result increases and its meaning for theory is significant. There is always the possibility of direct replication, that is, the repetition of the experiment under the same conditions, except that it is performed at a different time and with different, although comparable, subjects. This type of replication adds credibility should its result be the same as the first experiment's. However, if a constant error were operating, or if the independent variables were arranged in such a manner as to have excluded certain factors which were important as influences on the dependent variable, simple replication would be of little value. Consequently, a different type of replication is necessary within the functionalist context.

"Systematic replication" refers to the repetition of an experiment where some of the independent variables (e.g., age, sex, deprivation time) are allowed to vary from the first experiment to test the strength and generality of the phenomenon under study. Should the results be the same in the systematic replication as in the original study, the authenticity of the result is greatly increased, compared particularly to a simple replication yielding the same results.

Systematic replication in simple learning studies with animals and humans is relatively easy to accomplish. In studies involving social behavior, however, the task is more difficult. In a series of studies on opinion change, extending from 1960 to 1965 (see References), the author attempted what might loosely be called systematic replication of various studies. The problem was to predict change in opinion either in the direction of a communication supporting, or of one opposing, a point of view concerning a topic of social interest, for example, racial integration of public facilities. A number of factors were presumed to affect the direction of opinion change, in addition to the order factor of the "pro" and "con" arguments presented to the subject. The degree of controversy of the topic of the communication, and the subject's interest in and familiarity with the topic, all seemed to influence the direction of opinion change. There also seemed to be little doubt that interest, controversy, and familiarity interacted in their effect on the direction of the opinion change. A series of replications were run which presumably would shed light on this interaction. Separate experiments were performed where the same procedure was used but where the degree of controversy was manipulated and one other variable introduced, such as degree of interest in the topic of the communication. The same situation could be handled by a rather straightforward factorial design where all independent variables could be manipulated at once and their independent effects examined separately. One variable, for example, familiarity with the topic of the communication, was varied in strength from study to study. Thus, when the direction of opinion change proved consistent over several studies with the variable conditions present, the strength of the result was more than the simple cumulative effect of a series of direct replications, or of a factorial design including all of the levels of the independent variables. However, there are still major differences between systematic replication of studies performed with human social problems in mind, and those involving animals, such as are described by Sidman (1960).

When an experimenter sets out to examine opinion change in a group of subjects he usually makes the following assumptions:

1. Whether or not the subject has an opinion about the topic, the conditions leading to such a state would have occurred outside the laboratory and would not be amenable to other than *ex post facto* study in his experiment.
2. Most likely, the subjects will already have learned what it means to change their opinion and how to read or listen to the communication which is presented to them.
3. The experimenter must use many subjects for his study because, since he is safe in believing that there will be many different conditions in the past histories of his subjects due to variation in personality and experience, he needs to produce a symmetrical if not normal distribution of various traits to get a meaningful test of his hypothesis.

The experimenter undoubtedly makes many more assumptions as well, but these will do for our purposes.

It seems to follow from this description of the usual opinion change research methodology, and from our description of Skinner's and Sidman's methodology, that neither would ever even attempt to make sense out of such studies. As we have seen, from Skinner's point of view, the important ingredients for predicting opinion change in the situation have already occurred when our opinion researcher began to do his study. The functionalists would be more interested in the nature of the assumptions the experimenter makes. Thus, the assumptions of Skinner's system and the methodology which follows from them disallow interest in such opinion-change experiments. It also follows, however, that one who strictly adheres to Skinner's system could never discover what, if anything, is discovered by the empirical *ex post facto* system just described. It may be possible to uncover important principles about opinion change, as contrasted to principles concerning opinion formation.

There is one very difficult problem in *ex post facto* social psychological research which Skinner's methodology avoids to a con-
siderable extent. It is the influence of the measuring instrument on
the subject and, hence, its interference with the identified independent variables. The problem is particularly acute in opinion and
attitude change research where it has been shown (Solomon, 1949;
Entwistle, 1961a, b; Lana, 1968) that, in many cases, the administration of a pretest in the form of a questionnaire to ascertain the
nature of a given opinion has as much effect on the subject's responses as any of the study's independent variables. The reason for
this is that the administration of a questionnaire to an adult on a
topic of social relevance is *a social situation in itself*. For example,
the subject might wonder why the experimenter wants his opinion
on such a topic, what responses his friends are putting on the questionnaire, etc. This behavioral "Heisenberg effect" is greatly minimized in a functional methodology such as Skinner's.

The Holists

The methodology of the holists must contain the following
characteristics in order to test the type of theory which we have discussed in Chapter Five:

1. The experiment must yield empirical evidence which con-
   firms an hypothesis regarding an integrated aspect of social
   behavior. What constitutes an integrated aspect of social
   behavior is, of course, a matter calling for some judgment on
   the part of the theorist. However, this may be made clearer
   by recalling Asch's line judging experiment on social conformity, discussed in Chapter Five. In that study, we remember, the subject altered his judgments of the length of
   the line segments, a relatively straightforward, easily measurable task, because of a complex pattern of social interaction between himself and his peers. The experiment cap-
   tures an episode of social influence which is meaningful in
   itself and does so by objective, empirical means. It is, in

short, an *"experimentum crucis"* of the early gestalt type done within the context of traditional social psychology.

2. The decisive test of an empirical hypothesis must not be based upon averages or other statistical entities which suggests a summing of the partial reactions of several individuals. This requirement is often violated by the holists, as we have seen, which points to a weakness in the adequacy of the assumptions and methodology of this approach. The reason for this weakness is that holistic theories are concerned mainly with behavior after it has occurred (ahistoricity), and not with the functional contingencies preceding its appearance. Once the behavior has occurred, the only possibility is to gather it for examination. In gathering this behavior, too many unknown factors have been operating on each individual subject for us to be able to depend upon the data generated by any one of them to support or refute a given hypothesis. Hence, statistics are necessary to make sense out of the data.

3. In the experimental situation, an active, life-like social environment must be created which, taken *in toto,* constitutes the independent variable as a configuration. Asch's experiment illustrates this point.

The functionalist, nonreductive approach to opinion and attitude research is quite different from the holistic methodology. In the typical opinion or attitude change study, the key variables in the environmental situation are already extraordinarily complex before the experimenter begins his environmental manipulations. The communication is administered to many subjects, all already having opinions and attitudes. Further, the subject is not placed in a situation which calls for his *direct* reaction to other people (as in the Asch study), which is, after all, the empirical core of social psychology. The subject has the relatively passive chore of responding in secrecy to questions on a piece of paper which he may or may not answer according to his true beliefs. There is no way to check immediately the validity of a single individual's response.

Probability Methodology

There is a third general methodology which, largely due to the inevitable limitations of their approaches, is occasionally found as part of the methodology used by the functionalists and the holists, but which can be taken as a separate method of procedure. This is what may be called the probability approach to research in social psychology, examples of which have already been discussed (e.g., the Lana studies). The approach has the following characteristics:

1. The dependent variable is examined by collecting averages through the use of some measuring device, such as a questionnaire or rating sheet, which is designed to record a response which presumably has been influenced by the independent variables impinging upon the subject.
2. There is a heavy dependence on selection of subjects to balance all relevant characteristics, rather than on experimental manipulation. Thus, selection of subjects is of extreme importance and much of the effort of this type of study is devoted to it.

The probability approach often permeates the other forms, for it is rarely possible to control initially all relevant social variables in order to structure an experiment. One of the greatest difficulties with this form of research, however, is that the dependent variable is usually a verbal product of long-term processes not manipulated by the experimenter, and which the subject may not be always truthful in voicing. Another problem is that, although the subject may respond in a truthful manner, his response still may not reflect the variable the experimenter is interested in, since the subject may have misunderstood the instructions, or responded at a different level of comprehension than was called for by the experimenter.

It is possible to minimize these difficulties by experimentally maximizing the probabilities against support of the study's principal hypothesis. That is, it is possible to maximize the probability of a Type I (radical) error at the expense of a Type II (conservative) error. If differences in independent variables are minimized in the experimental procedure, which according to the hypothesis should yield a difference in response in the dependent variable, then results which show differences among the various experimental groups are even more supportive of the hypothesis than had these differences been maximized. For example, in the situation where controversy of a topic of communication is considered an independent variable, two experiments may be designed such that the second utilizes two degrees of controversy which are closer together than in an initial experiment where all other factors are the same. Should the results of the second experiment show differences in the dependent variable (e.g., opinion change) similar to the results in the first experiment where the degrees of controversy for the two experimental groups were greater, then there is stronger evidence that differences in degree of controversy yield differences in opinion change *caeteris paribus*. There is always the possibility of increasing the probability of a Type II error in an experimental design by "stacking" the manipulations of the independent variables against the hypothesis of the study, and thus being more assured of arriving at a conservative conclusion.

Use of Statistics in Social Psychological Research

At least as early as the beginning 1940's, and continuing with varying bursts of enthusiasm to the present day, criticism of the use of statistics in dealing with experimental psychological data has come from various sources. The early gestalt psychologists objected to the sometimes elaborate statistical analyses performed by behavioristically oriented psychologists, for example, of the Hull school. In this case, the criticism was consistent with the general gestalt orientation regarding the total environmental situation of an organism. (We have already discussed part of this problem in Chapter Five.) Later, behaviorists of the Skinnerian school were to object rigorously to this use of statistics on the ground that it begged the question of controlling the organism, that is, of shaping its behavior so that most relevant variables were controlled. Thus, no "averaging" technique via statistical analysis would be necessary. The elaborate use of statistics was seen as an admission of failure to control relevant variables experimentally. Finally, at least one mathematician (Hogben, 1957) has chided psychologists for improper application of statistical tools to the data of psychological experimentation. We may assume that the criticism has some basis in fact; that is, that some psychologists have been guilty of misuse or overuse of statistical tools to the point where the data have been separated from their organic base. It is also true, however, that one can indicate misuse or overuse of tools and concepts within the other theoretical orientations of psychology as well. We need to examine briefly what the best use of these statistical tools has been, and whether criticism of any sort is valid for these instances.

In 1957, Hogben wrote an extremely interesting history of statistics which included an analysis of the general use of statistics in various fields, including psychology. He divided his exposition into four types of statistical activities. These are:

1. The calculus of error, which refers to the classic notion of the assignment of probability in games of chance. Observations are combined to provide the best estimate of an assumed true value of some aspects of nature, which then can be demonstrated as an independent law.

2. The calculus of aggregates, which refers to the establishment of similar estimates in subsensory or subatomic particles, as in physics and genetics.

3. The calculus of exploration, which is concerned with regression and hence factor analysis. It is deemed least sufficient of the four calculi in maintaining consistency with the probability assumptions of classical theory.

4. The calculus of judgment, which refers to the entire process of statistical inference via tests of significance.

The main difficulties in using these calculi, as Hogben sees them, lie within the framework of exploration and judgment, which are the two most important statistical activities for psychological research. Any statistics developed for inference and exploration must adhere to the principle of randomization, which, in turn, must either be demonstrated conclusively *before* the use of a related statistic, or be assured by a mechanical procedure. Even if assured by a mechanical procedure, however, one is not guaranteed that nature will conform to the principle of randomization in the relevant distribution. The experimenter who would make a statistical inference is in difficult straits, according to Hogben, since the first possibility is rarely present in the social sciences. Hogben also notes that statistics of the inferential variety must be used within the framework of repetition over an infinite population. All of this must be specified before, rather than after, the distribution of events has been empirically described. This latter point condemns the hypothesis-testing procedure of much of American experimental psychology derived from R. A. Fisher's theory of inference.

Hogben states:

If we abandon the claim to assign a probability to the truth of a particular verdict as inconsistent with a behaviorist approach, we must regard a calculus of judgments as a prescription for a collective discipline of interpretation in contradistinction to a sanction for individual conviction. We may still concede the possibility of building an edifice of new theory on foundations more secure than the infinite hypothetical population; but we have then to ask: what useful role can such a calculus fulfill in the biological or social sciences? For my part I should hesitate to say *none at all;* but we shall be wise to refrain from indulging in unjustifiable expectations about the situations in which it may be helpful to enquiry (1957, p. 468).

And again:

If it is proper to say that statistics is the science of averages, we should be hesitant about enlisting statistics in experimental enquiry before asking: is the answer to our question usefully expressable in terms of an average? Otherwise, undue reliance on statistics must impede the march of science by encouraging us to ask useless questions or to refrain from asking the most useful ones (Hogben, 1957, p. 469).

When statistical procedure is invoked, we are asking questions which are concerned with: (1) a rough classification of individuals along some dimension(s) for simple taxonomic purposes; (2) arriving at a solid understanding of the laws of individual behavior. The first for Hogben is simply "a piece of social accountancy," and can be accomplished with statistics derived from the heritage of Neyman. The second is accomplished neither by Fisherian nor Neymanian methods. For our purposes, it is not necessary to distinguish these methods, which the reader is encouraged to examine in Hogben's book. Hogben goes on to say that these "screening devices" have a seductive effect on many experimenters which encourages them to avoid certain fundamental issues in the field.

Yet, it seems that psychologists have put statistics to uses that are more sophisticated than Hogben realizes. Many psychologists see the usual use of statistical inferential procedures in experimental design as the best substitute for experimental control. They feel that statistically derived "social accountancy" may often precede deep understanding of individual behavior. We shall expand upon this slightly below.

Another criticism of statistical inference made along lines similar to Hogben's is that of Sidman (1960), in his *Tactics of Scientific Research*. Sidman's criticism is a fundamental one. He argues that there is a desirable alternative to the position that the search for truth is best pursued through the use of statistical inference, whereby the reduction of chance factors in observations relevant to various hypotheses is the *sine qua non* of progress. For Sidman, the testing of an hypothesis is less important than careful empirical control of independent variables associated with the observation of some dependent variable. He makes a point, similar to Hogben's, that there is great difficulty in determining the shapes of the distributions of the parent population of the experimental sample, or of meaningfully choosing the appropriate test statistic, with all that that implies.

If chance is associated with ignorance of factors influencing the dependent variable, psychologists are making a mistake in utilizing procedures such as statistics which are predicated on chance factors as the major criterion associated with progress in experimentation.

"Science is presumably dedicated to stamping out ignorance, but statistical evaluation of data against a baseline whose characteristics are determined by unknown variables constitutes a passive acceptance of ignorance" (Sidman, 1960, p. 45). It is extremely difficult to follow Sidman's logic in this last statement and, indeed, one may wonder whether he was completely serious in making it. However, it is clear that the use of any technique based in part upon ignorance, when others *free from this taint* are available, is most assuredly contrary to the ideals of science. At least in social psychology, these techniques are not now available. Sidman would most likely hold that, if that is the case, we should be searching for them. Perhaps we should. However, he also recognizes that functional, nonhypothesis-testing, nonstatistical techniques work best with phenomena which are reversible (e.g., learning, unlearning), and have great difficulty with phenomena which are not. By and large, group and individual behavior in human beings has seemed to be extremely difficult to reverse, unless it was superficially acquired initially. It is extremely difficult to change an attitude once formed, much less change it back to its original form, but it is easier to do this with opinions on topics relatively unimportant to an individual. In these circumstances, the cataloguing and weighting of independent variables relevant to some dependent variable may yield more information about the particular phenomenon than other approaches.

In the final analysis, the use of statistics in experimental design is almost synonymous with the desire to assign a probability to an empirically based conclusion. Since all empirically based conclusions have at least an implicit probability associated with them, a criticism of the use of statistics for this purpose is certainly invalid. In the case of the more complicated and sophisticated uses of statistically based experimental design, where there is a heavy dependence upon statistical manipulation to draw conclusions, a danger exists only when this statistical manipulation is utilized *instead* of empirical manipulation (i.e., control) of the relevant variables. It is, of course, relatively simple for an experimenter to fall into the habit of utilizing statistical techniques in place of searching for empirical ones to establish higher probabilities associated with each conclusion. However, the burden of demonstration at any given point in the history of an experimental problem lies with the experimenter who would empirically control variables, rather than with one who uses statistical treatment for want of a better tool with which to proceed.

Repeated Measures

One of the main problems within the statistical framework of examining results from experiments concerns the generation of correlated measures from repeated measures on the same individual or from multiple criteria. Hogben sees the problem as deriving, in part, from the universality of the Neyman approach to statistical inference in psychological research. The problem is especially acute in experiments in social psychology where before-and-after measures are used, in drug studies where repeated dosages are utilized on the same organisms, and in learning studies where measures of progress on the same organisms over time are necessary. Until recently (Winer, 1962; Lana and Lubin, 1963), this mensurative problem has generally been ignored by methodologists and by writers of statistical texts for psychologists. Although various statistical solutions are available to deal with this problem (see Lana and Lubin, 1963), there seems to be a paucity of empirical solutions, which would be preferable in the long run. How, for example, is it possible to know whether opinion change over several administrations of various persuasive communications is a result of an additive, multiplicative, or other relation existing as a cumulative effect of these communications, or is a result of factors associated more with the daily lives of the human organisms? In short, how does one separate out these factors by empirical manipulation? With a statistical technique a solution is possible, but only after very fundamental assumptions are made about the nature of the empirical data. In one case, the methodology, and in the other, closeness of fit between technique of analysis and subject matter, is lacking. In the history of social psychological research, there seems presently to be an advantage in statistical analysis, save perhaps for a few highly specific problems. There seems to be little doubt, however, that careful control by experimental manipulation is more desirable in the long run.

Mathematical Models

Although the use of probability mathematics to assign probabilities to experimental results involves a search for a mathematical function which "fits" a collection of empirical data, the use of mathematical models in psychology involves a somewhat different orientation. The fitting of mathematical models to human social data is usually a search for mathematical functions useful for predicting social behavior. The mathematical function that "fits" the data consistently becomes a form of law. It explains the relevant phenomena by enabling one to predict behavior. Probability mathematics may, in turn, be used to assign a probability to the likelihood that a particular mathematical function fits a particular class of data, but then the problem becomes the same as that discussed above.

The use of mathematical models has enjoyed a certain popularity in social psychological theorizing, and we shall examine one such attempt to illustrate their uses in this area. It is necessary to mention that modern mathematical models used in social psychology are concerned with fitting only a certain kind of data with a mathematical function, and that there is rarely an attempt to generalize applicability even to a few other forms of social behavior.

Anderson (1959) has written an equation which may serve as a model for predicting order effects in opinion change when two different communications are presented to subjects in *ab* and *ba* orders. From observations in various other studies, Anderson developed the following formula for predicting opinion change within the framework of a before-after situation:

$$X_1 = X_0 + S(C - X_0) \qquad (1)$$

where X_0 is the opinion of the subject before presentation of a communication;

X_1 is the opinion of the subject after presentation of the com-
    munication;

C is the fixed point of the communication on the relevant
    opinion continuum;

S is a coefficient of proportionality corresponding to the sub-
    ject's susceptibility to the communication.

From the above, Anderson derives a formula for predicting a
recency effect (change) of opinion toward the position advocated by
the communication presented second. It is assumed that $C_b = C_a$,
which simply indicates that the position advocated by one of the
communications is further up the opinion continuum. The formula is:

$$X_{ab} - X_{ba} = S_a S_b (C_b - C_a). \qquad (2)$$

The expression on the left side of the equation is defined as the
order effect. It represents the difference in opinion change between
subjects receiving the *ab* order and subjects receiving the *ba* order.
Should equation *(1)* be satisfied in the empirical situation, a recency
effect will be obtained [equation *(2)*]. (The reader is encouraged to
consult Anderson [1959] for the detailed argument.) Anderson
then cites evidence that the propositions work with actual data.
Since equation *(1)* represents a linear relationship existing between the initial opinion and opinion after presentation of the communication, Anderson's work is an attempt to fit a simple straight
line function to certain opinion change phenomena. There is, however, no attempt to utilize the equation for any other type of social
data. It may develop that the function is more general than intended
in this study, but he intentionally strictly limits its use to the phenomenon under immediate study. Thus, in terms of our previous
analysis and observations, the fitting of mathematical models to
empirical data is closest to the functional-reductive approach of explanation of social activity. It suffers from its difficulties, and benefits
from its strongpoints. In model fitting, the emphasis is placed upon
the final obtained function and its fit, rather than upon the initial
empirical control of relevant environmental and organismic variables.

chapter

9

Conclusions and Perspective

One of the most important points emerging from the last several chapters is the necessity for keeping separate research strategy on the one hand, and theoretical orientation on the other. Quite often the two are confused, perhaps in part because the theoreticians themselves make little or no effort to maintain the distinction. The problem becomes particularly acute when we are dealing with social psychological theories, since the relevant variables represent extremely complicated sets of environmental and individual conditions. A research strategy always implies a methodology which may or may not be consistent with a given theoretical position. It is true, however, that a particular strategy for studying social behavior can imply certain theoretical assumptions regarding the subject matter, if research strategy alone is articulated by the researcher. We have found this to occur particularly within the framework of traditional behaviorism and its modern derivatives.

Quite often, what I have called "fractionated approaches" to specific sub-problems within the totality of social psychology are more influenced by the method of research procedure than by an articulated theoretical orientation on the part of the researcher. The extraordinary difficulty in constructing a promising theory for explaining all or most social activity has led theorists to concentrate on segments of this activity. This, in turn, has produced a concentration on method, as opposed to theory, in the general approach to the problem. The concern has been to make some sense, at least empirically, out of various types of social phenomena, such as opinion change or the nature of leadership in small groups, rather than out of the entire social context, which would allow the possibility for successful prediction. To some extent, the fractionated approaches have succeeded in predicting relevant phenomena, but they have rarely supported any inclusive theory of social behavior. In any case, as suggested throughout this book, there are no logical grounds whereby a successful methodology (one that leads to correct prediction) can supply a theoretical structure to tie together the empirically predicted events. Of course, one may do without any theory at all, and instead collect a series of functional relations which hold among various environmental and response contingencies, so as to produce a catalogue of behavior. If one does this, however, most likely there will be aspects which would not fit into any functional contingency and therefore would be excluded from consideration. Any explanatory power which a formally or semiformally constructed theory may actually have for dealing with the data also would be automatically excluded, since functional contingencies *per se* can never lead to theory.

The decision to pursue a strictly functional program of research, devoid of any attempts to postulate theoretical entities or aids in theorizing, usually reflects the researcher's implicit or explicit belief that the terms of social psychology eventually will be reducible to those of a discipline with less complex units, such as physiology. Some psychologists (e.g., Jessor, 1958) have argued that there may be logical impossibilities preventing psychological theories from being reduced to physiological ones. Jessor points out that the fact that environmental variables, which appear as structural elements in psychological theories, are not includable in any current theories of physiology. However, this is not a valid argument against the point that future physiological theories might contain appropriate references to nonorganic environmental variables. Certainly, it remains possible that future physiological theories may include environmental variables which function in prediction. It seems that the only formal restriction against reduction of this sort stems from the validity and nature of the *a priori* in causal thinking and simply from reasonable thought in general. I have indicated in various sections of this book that several men have demonstrated the logical impossibility of reducing our ideas *about* explanation (i.e., theories) to the observation of empirical contingencies, no matter how complex these contingencies may be. Beyond this objection, there is no logical reason why a great deal of psychological principles now and in the future may not be reducible to some of the derivatives of current or future physiological or other theories. However, there is an immediate need to think about psychological problems, especially those of social psychology, in terms of units of analysis and structures of theory which are molar in nature and which are not now reducible to other terms, even within general psychology. Consequently, problems in social psychology which, for example, bear a relation to the nature and use of language may resist solution by means of functional analysis, and may yield more easily to analysis through the use of research and theoretical ideas generated by a holistic approach.

In a functional system such as Skinner's, we have noted that the process of inference depends upon the observation of consistent sets of events identifiable in the environment and existing in a relationship of constant conjunction with certain responses of the organism. The all-important inference to unobserved instances is based on a process well articulated by Hume, but which Skinner does not accept as valid. However, Skinner is not dogmatic concerning the exclusive application of his system to social activity as this passage indicates:

> To apply our analysis to the phenomena of the group is an excellent way to test its adequacy, and if we are able to account for the behavior of people in groups without using any new term or presupposing any new process or principle, we shall have revealed a promising simplicity in the data. This does not mean that the social sciences will then inevitably state their generalizations in terms of individual behavior, since another level of description may also be valid and may well be more convenient (Skinner, 1953, p. 298).

However one justifies the validity of such an inferential process, it is, as we have seen, by far the safest way to make inferences concerning empirical events. Only the constant conjunction of specified observable events is noted. Expectations of events are based on these observations rather than on assumptions concerning psychological or other entities presumed to be operating as influences. In daily life, we successfully use the idea of causation as production. When it can be so used in scientific work, it usually is. The idea of cause as producer is implied in the classical theories of Galileo and Newton in physics, as well in the hypothetico-deductive theories of Hull (1943) in psychology. Whenever any doubt arises as to the productive capacity of a presumed cause, one may safely conclude that he has at least observed a constant conjunction of environmental conditions and organismic responses which have occurred over many instances in time. This "safety valve" is particularly useful in the social sciences where the idea of causation as production remains a difficult notion to apply to the seemingly endless variety of relationships existing among relevant environmental and behavioral variables. However, simply because a system of psychological explanation is most conservative in its claims about the nature of human activity, this does not mean that it is necessarily the correct way or the most promising way of attempting to explain such activity. There is no way of avoiding indefinitely the introduction of theoretical entities, and, therefore, of integrated theory, as the best vehicle for explaining human or any other kind of animal activity. However, within the framework of any scientific system, the validity of either a functional, conceptual, or other form of system which leads to a specific formal or informal theory, must be tested eventually by empirical evidence. Hence, the form of validation for any explanation of human activity is, finally, the ability to predict relevant behavior. The general form of scientific inquiry as outlined above has been invariable throughout the entire history of scientific enterprise, although there has been a cyclical emphasis on theoretical entities and on simple empirical contingencies.

The functional view of explanation in contemporary social psychology was a successful reaction against the apparently bankrupt theorizing prevalent in the late nineteenth and early twentieth century. It has served its purpose for data gathering in social psychology and needs to give way to other forms of analysis.

Creativity and the Creative Genius

As complex phenomena occurring between two or more individuals, "creativity" seems to be neither analyzable nor reducible to simpler phenomena by functional means. A glance at Skinner's ideas on the subject is enlightening. He likens the "creative genius" to the individual who, through the given medium of expression, has produced a product which more people over a longer period of time have found reinforcing, compared to the products of others using the same medium. "Reinforcement" is used by Skinner in this context to indicate that people will repeatedly make some set of verbal or other responses in order to "consume" the object in question, say a painting. That is, they will go to see the painting repeatedly in an art gallery, perhaps attempt to buy it, say that they like it, will feel good or feel elevated when they look at it, etc. The individual artist who can create many of this type of painting is declared a "universal genius" by his admirers, although it is doubtful that they would accept Skinner's analysis. With this definition of creative genius, it is easily demonstrable that a cheesemaker or a volleyball player can qualify for the honor. Skinner perhaps would not dispute this, but he would certainly mention that, although painter, cheesemaker, and volleyball player may all be creative geniuses, most people in a given society hold the subject matter of their various skills in differential repute. There are different values attached to each of the endeavors. Another set of reinforcements must be introduced in order to explain why these different values exist, but this is another problem.

Skinner's conception of what we mean by a creative genius does, in fact, contain a great deal of the notion of what most people mean when they assign this status to an artist, a cheesemaker or a volleyball star. However, the question of, for example, what it is that a given artist does when he paints that makes his paintings re-inforcing to many people is the more important question. Hence, Skinner's discussion of the concept of creativity, limited as it is to studying reinforcing properties of behavior *not particularly relevant* to the product of creativity, can never deal with "newness," an attri-bute which generally is included in a definition of the term. We have chosen only one pole on the continuum of creativity, that is, the genius, but the analysis works for any degree of this attribute. For Skinner, newness is new combinations of already known elements. One might make some sense out of what makes a painting or book creatively new and worthwhile by engaging in a verbal, that is, con-ceptual, analysis of the relevant objects and processes. (This might be more meaningful if we deal with a novel rather than with a painting, which may not be so amenable to our tool of verbal analysis.) Thus, the relevance of Skinner's analysis of creativity through reinforcement concepts once again reduces to whether lan-guage is totally or principally understandable in these reinforcement terms. We have concluded in Chapter Four that it is not so totally reducible. The argument remains the same for the concept of crea-tivity. One may also observe that in Skinner's argument individual creativity eventually must be predictable. This would not follow, however, if one's definition of "newness" should differ from Skinner's.

It would follow from Skinner's position that art over the years is cumulative in its effect, in the same way we believe science to be cumulative. For example, we understand Caravaggio's techniques for artistic reinforcement, but also have modern ones. While this way of thinking about creative genius is undoubtedly uncommon, it con-tains some of what we really mean by this term and, therefore, what we mean when we talk of the various ways in which we are affected by art, literature or, for that matter, a good cheese. Should this type of analysis be applied to the quality of a painting, however, its suc-cess as a reinforcement mediator would eventually yield a conclusion of the following sort: People, for whatever reasons, react positively (are reinforced) to triangles more than to any other shape, and to red more than to any other color and, hence, the artist who paints red triangles is more likely to elicit approach responses towards his painting than one who concentrates upon circularity in varying shades of the green portion of the spectrum. Thus, a functional reinforcement analysis must examine the reaction of individuals to the various elements of a painting. These elements could be more complex than triangularity and redness. They could also be people and pastoral scenes, for example.

In *Walden II,* Skinner's novel about the possibility of constructing a society using the principal of positive reinforcement, he bravely suggests that not only is the technique available for building such a society, but that new values will somehow be a byproduct of the technique. When *Walden II* has been discussed in various seminars, the brighter students seemed to divide rather violently in their appraisal of it. One group tended to be strongly convinced that the Principle of Positive Reinforcement made a good deal more sense than any other grand solution to the problems of society to which they had been exposed. The other group tended to be rather repelled by what they thought would be the production of a bland society of people living in an orderly but dull world. A friend of mine was upset because there seems to be no possibility that such a society could produce a Casey Stengel! Without attempting a detailed analysis of the novel, we may examine some of the implications of life in a society where the principal mechanism of structure is through the arrangement of the environment of the individual such that patterns of responses are conditioned by positive reinforcement. The development of values emerging in such an individual would have to come from relationships between him and his environment which are not possible to arrange through positive or negative reinforcement. A demonstration of the truth of this proposition is made in Chapters Two, Three and Four, which contain a similar argument. Values are independent both of the data to which they refer and of the method used to collect that data. As indicated earlier, the functional approach to human activity is both the method of analysis and the method by which one changes and modifies this activity. However, it also seems true that much of society's work, including almost all of the drudgery associated with the more mechanical tasks of teaching, can be made easier by various applications of the method of positive reinforcement. Skinner and others have already demonstrated the extraordinary success in certain areas that one may achieve using these functional techniques (e.g., programmed learning).

Functional-Reductive and Holistic Theories

In the other type of functional theory of social behavior, where theoretical entities or processes are postulated, such as Helson's concept of adaptation, some of the problems that arise are of a different type than those we have been describing. Helson's notion of adaptation (Chapter Four) was advanced as a dynamic property of the organism useful in understanding phenomena as diverse as hunger and social affiliation. It was suggested that these phenomena, as well as many others, are aspects of human activity which are most explainable by an equilibrium concept such as that of adaptation. However, in social relationships usually described by terms such as love, humor, and conversational repartee, the concept seems to be of little use. These relationships seem to involve verbal conceptual elements which are at least partially irrelevant to equilibrium concepts. The phenomenon of wanting to meet new people can scarcely fit an equilibrium model of explanation, unless by tortuous modification of the original. Social exploration outside of the individual's already constituted groups requires an idea different from adaptation. Helson's idea might be applied to the case of social exploration of a prospective member introduced to a group, in that the exploration might serve to "neutralize" the new member. Information gained about him would either coincide with the group's principles, and therefore he would be acceptable, or it would not, and the group would act to remove him. In either case, one might argue that an equilibrium would have been established in the group as a result of the exploration and, therefore, in the individuals composing it. But how does the idea of adaptation help to explain the behavior of an individual who moves to a new city to seek new kinds of people?

It is important to make a distinction between the *form* of explanation suggested by Helson, that is, that some kind of equilibrium (adaptation) is the explanatory principal behind social as well as simpler forms of activity, and the idea that adaptation is a successful concept for explaining various kinds of simple phenomena. Further, it is important to note that because social activity might be reducible to simpler phenomena, it is not necessarily explained by adaptation. Helson most likely would support the first contention rather than the second.

In contrast to the difficulties which we have encountered with the ability of theories to explain social phenomena, the holistic theories seem to be relatively free from problems involving assumptions and potentials for generalization to social and other complex forms of human activity. However, despite this advantage, the holistic position encounters difficulty in generating a unique methodological approach which would succeed in maintaining the assumptions of the general approach and, at the same time, yield empirical information relevant to theory and useful for prediction. Although it seems clear that social activity is extraordinarily complex, there seems to be no experimental (observational) method that may be directly applied which both preserves the complexity of the empirical phenomena and yields checkable predictions at the same time. The stark simplicity of the functional approach seems impeccable as a research strategy, if not as a theoretical orientation. In comparison to holistic, functional methodology is much more closely related to the fundamental idea of classical (Galilean) scientific endeavor which states that analysis must proceed synthesis. Analysis implies reduction of some aspects of the original phenomena to more manageable units, whether this reduction be a temporary or a permanent measure. As a necessary component of scientific analysis, reduction is more easily supported by the functional than by the holistic point of view, especially with respect to the complex phenomena of social activity.

It is apparently impossible to reconcile the differences in both theory and strategy between the holistic and functional points of view. In the past, these differences have been interpreted as temporary, with a high probability that they would be resolved sometime in the future. It is more likely that the two ways of looking at behavior are logically separate, as we have attempted to indicate above. The separation is particularly noticeable, and perhaps most important, when the subject matter of study is the social activity of human beings. It seems clear that some problems of social activity are best conceived and handled by a functional approach, while others await a holistic examination. Thus, a "division of labor" between the two approaches allows a differential focus on various problems which arise in the social situation. Of course, this division only temporarily solves the problem of explanation.

Difficulties of Integrating Theories

An example of the difficulties of integrating the various functional and holistic theories can be seen by examining four major ways of explaining the order effects of opposed persuasive communications on opinion change among adult subjects. The problem is to provide an explanation for the fact that, under certain circumstances, the first of two successive opposed communications on a given topic is more effective in changing the opinion of adult subjects and that, under other circumstances, the second communication is more effective. In all studies of this phenomenon, the "pro" and "con" communications are counterbalanced to allow for measurement of a position (order) effect.

There are three theories within the framework of functional explanation used to explain the order effects yielded by many experimental situations. In one, the principal element determining either a "primacy" effect (success of the first of two communications in changing opinion) or a "recency" effect (success of the second communication) is the position of a reinforcement within the persuasive situation (McGuire, 1957; Rosnow and Russell, 1963; Rosnow and Lana, 1965). The general idea is that the communication ("pro" or "con") closest in time to the reinforcement will yield opinion change in the direction advocated by that communication. This is an application of the old law of effect. The reinforcement need not be relevant to the content of the communication or to the context of the experiment. In the experimental situation just cited, if one postulates the existence of a relevant process of equilibrium such as cognitive dissonance (Festinger, 1957), or of the need for sensory variation (Schultz, 1963), then changing opinion in one direction or the other (primacy or recency) depends upon some automatic balancing mechanism operating in the organism. For example, Schultz's principal hypothesis is that when an individual is exposed to a topic for the first time, the first communication is perceived as novel and mediates increased cortical activity. A second (opposed) communication on the same topic provides little activation compared with the first communication and, hence, in order to maintain activity (the need for sensory variation), the individual reacts in accordance with the position advocated by the initial communication. Therefore, a primacy effect should result. It sometimes does, and it sometimes does not. Schultz has listed other hypotheses to account for order effects among persuasive communications in related situations. However, we need not enumerate them here since we are interested only in the form of the explanation. Cognitive dissonance theorists would postulate the operation of a need to reduce dissonance arising from the successive presentation of opposed communications under conditions of the subject's commitment to one alternative or the other, but an equilibrium process would still be involved.

The reinforcement interpretation is functional in pairing reinforcement with opinion change, but it postulates no operative process controlling the phenomenon. The cognitive dissonance and sensory variation interpretations postulate equilibrious processes which control opinion change. In the reinforcement and sensory variation interpretations, the content of the communication is almost irrelevant to the process of opinion change, except that it must be coherent and novel in the latter case. Since opinion change implies a cognitive and, therefore, a verbal process, these positions essentially ignore the complications and meaning that this fact entails. Of course, one may be able to predict cognitive change from observing the noncognitive aspects of the process. However, order effects have not been fully explained by any theory. In the case of cognitive dissonance theory, the subject must perceive discrepancies existing between certain elements of his own opinions and beliefs, and those expressed by the communications. This implies that the meaning, that is, the content of the communications, is important in opinion change. The dissonance (disequilibrium) established by this discrepancy, although cognitive in nature, is presumed to follow a cycle of increase and decrease, similar to various physiological activities such as hunger and thirst. We have discussed the implications and possibilities of this kind of model in Chapter Seven. However, the cognitive dissonance position does represent a middle ground between the reinforcement and sensory variation positions on the one hand, and the more conceptually derived attempt at explaining order effects in persuasive communications, namely set theory, on the other hand.

The set interpretation of order effect phenomena suggests that an individual confronted with new material will form a "set" (that is, an organization of cognitive concepts) consistent with the information and, hence, the direction of the argument of the communication first presented. He will tend to continue to react consistently with the communication presented first, rather than with the one presented second. During the presentation of the second communication, cognitive organization will have already occurred which will have rendered this communication ineffective in influencing opinion. Of course, if the subject is already familiar with the topic of the communication, this analysis is not applicable.

It seems clear that there is little possibility that the set analysis will ever be reduced to the reinforcement or the sensory variation analysis. No reconciliation is possible. One depends upon the internal, meaningful structure of the opinion process, namely what the subject thinks and how this thinking is organized on a conscious, rational, or conceptual level (or whatever term of this sort one prefers). The other two depend upon a process external to the conceptual one, namely an equilibrium process having nothing to do with the verbal, conscious, or rational content of the opinion or communication. It is true, however, that the cognitive dissonance explanation seems to combine the major elements of both types of theories. But, clearly, there can be no rational or empirical assimilation of the other explanations of order effects. Because neither the set nor the reinforcement theories have adequately explained the relevant empirical data (see Lana, 1964c), their explanations are applicable only to certain small segments of the already highly specialized problem of order effects. Set theory is relevantly applied only when the individual has had no previous exposure to the topic of the communication, which extremely limits its possibilities of explanation when one is interested in widely discussed social problems. The reinforcement theory is limited to situations where a concept of reinforcement, that is, reward or punishment, can definitely be located in the opinion change situation. This is no small task since in the actual process of opinion change found in daily life, people are involved in the highly complex verbal polemics usually associated with any interesting social issue.

In short, the problem lies in the basic assumptions which these two types of theories make about some important characteristics of social phenomena. The functionalists assume that these characteristics are reducible to the terms of general psychology and eventually, perhaps, to the terms of physiology and physics. The holists assume that they are organized, conceptual, and nonreducible in nature, and must be examined in their totality, that is, *in situ,* using concepts which are essentially the same as those they seek to elucidate.

Is there anything we can conclude about what we actually *know* to be the general nature of social activity? Are there reasonably fruitful ways of examining this activity so as to avoid the pitfalls of using the assumptions and methodology of any one of these approaches to solve problems which, by the very manner in which the problems are conceived, cannot possibly yield solution? Perhaps.

In all the phenomena which we call social, there are factors influencing various activities which are not part of the verbal, cognitive content of a conscious, "social" human being. For example, the following are factors influencing opinion change which psychologists have studied: the order of presentation of opposing arguments, the degree of controversiality of the topic involved, the prestige of the communicator, the degree of emotional involvement of the subject with the topic, the mechanical means of transmitting the communication, and the style or form of the communication. The list could be greatly extended. The subject is not consciously aware that these factors are affecting the way he responds to communications, and the way he changes his opinions. There seems to be no question that these variables do, in fact, influence opinion and, perhaps, attitude change. The research literature is rich in support of this general point. However, it is also obvious that much of what we mean by having and changing an opinion or attitude occurs at a conscious level. That is, people think, verbalize, and argue with themselves and with one another and may come to a change in opinion on the basis of fact and reasoning (or they *believe* the change is made on this basis). The research literature indicates a paucity of studies involving these latter types of processes, however. A notable exception is the work by McGuire (1960) on the use of syllogistic reasoning in responding to persuasive communications.

In McGuire's interesting studies, he investigated, among other things, whether a person's beliefs on related topics tend to be consistent with one another, that is, tend not to contradict the pattern required by the rules of formal logic. The individual is "thinking logically" to the extent that his belief in a given proposition follows logically from his beliefs on related propositions. McGuire constructs a model which he uses to examine a subject's logical consistency in various experimental situations. His basic paradigm is the following: if a person assents to both of two propositions (a and b) or if he assents to a third (k), then to be logical he must also assent to a fourth (c). In symbolic form:

$$(\quad (a \quad b) \quad k) \rightarrow c.$$

He gives the following example:

(a) A major nuclear war would result in violent death to at least half of the earth's population.
(b) A major nuclear war will occur within the next ten years.
(k) Factors other than nuclear war are going to result in violent

death to at least half the earth's population within the next ten years.

(*c*) At least half the earth's population will meet violent death within the next ten years (McGuire, 1960, p. 68).

The person's belief on any given issue can be determined by asking him to which statements he assents, and examining his responses for consistency against the logically sound paradigm. Experimental procedures were employed to disguise the fact that the experimenter was looking for logical consistency in the subject's reactions to questionnaires containing statements such as those listed above. Logically consistent persuasive communications were used, and logically consistent opinion change was noted.

The area of persuasive communication and opinion and attitude formation and change is one which, perhaps more than any other within the structure of social psychology, tends towards a research emphasis on nonconscious factors and their influence. However, the same apparent dichotomy (conscious-nonconscious) in research may be noted within the study of mass communication (Schramm, 1962) and group dynamics (Steiner, 1964). Undoubtedly, much of social activity is determined by these nonconscious factors. But perhaps some of the impasses one encounters in well-worked areas of research are due, at least in part, to their being overemphasized. Even the study of verbal behavior can become locked in a functional-reductive grip. The point is that we cannot afford a continuing attempt to reduce these verbal-cognitive processes to the terms associated with "nonconscious" factors, either within ongoing research or within the working ideas for future research. We must deal with them on their own terms, as increasingly more psychologists (e.g., Koch, 1964, 1956; Nissen, 1954) are insisting upon. Some psychologists seem to be moving towards a concern for more complicated units of analysis gleaned from the empirical situation itself, rather than from the assumptive base of a given theory or research strategy. Presumably, the construction of theory will follow the results of these empirically-based leads.

Psychology and Literature

It follows from a renewed interest in more complicated units of study that fictional literature has come closer to psychological science as means for understanding human behavior than it has for many years. I am referring to the possibility of fictional literature functioning in a manner that will allow for more accurate prediction of human behavior, that is, after one has grasped the author's system of explanation. Obviously, one may legitimately argue that the function, purpose, meaning, etc., of fictional literature are much more than just described, particularly since we are speaking of universally applicable literature. However, just as there are successful and unsuccessful psychological theories, these qualifications have parallels in literary enterprise. It seems obvious that one area of common interest existing between the fictional writer and the psychologist is that involving social activity. To say that literary analysis of social situations will eventually be reducible to the terms of psychology is useless, both for the current understanding of social activity and for the promise of a future development. It is difficult to conceive that a hypothetical man who is conversant neither with the science of psychology nor the art of Dostoyevsky, but is articulate and perceptive, would not understand, in the sense of being able to *predict* more accurately, as much or more about human social activity by reading the Russian's novels than by reading all of the social psychology books ever written.

Unlike Koch (1964), I do not believe that American psychologists are to be chided for this, for they have chosen a perfectly legitimate, and somewhat successful, general approach to the problem. However, it also seems clear that they may need to come closer to the fictional unit of analysis than they have previously been comfortable with. Lewin has been in this tradition, but he never provided the methodological power that the functional-reductive theorists have in the past. R. S. Peters (1958) provides a particularly relevant example of this point. If we meet a friend on the corner and ask him where he is going, and he answers that he is going to get some tobacco, we have the basis for a fairly accurate prediction about what he will do in the next few minutes. We know there is a tobacco shop across the street, and we know that he knows this. We then predict he will cross the street, enter the shop, buy some tobacco, and leave within a short period of time. We can, of course, check our prediction quite easily. Also, our prediction will be better than one based upon a detailed physiological, functional, or psychoanalytic analysis. In this case, analysis of his cognitive behavior, that is, of its content and *meaning,* allowed us to make a correct, and perhaps highly useful, prediction. We have short-circuited the analytic processes that the physiologist or behaviorist would make, given the same situation. The point is that there are many areas of human activity, especially in the communicative social area, where this cognitive analysis is more *predictively* useful than other types of approaches.

That Skinner would object to the above analysis is evident from his comments on the analysis of the "smile":

That the final identification of the stimulus pattern called a smile would be much more complicated and time-consuming than the identification of a smile in daily life does not mean that scientific observation neglects some important approach available to the layman. The difference is that the scientist must identify a stimulus with respect to the behavior of someone else. He cannot trust his own personal reaction (Skinner, 1953, p. 301).

But the objectivity of the scientist is not the question here. Rather, it is the ability of *anyone* to make a consistently *successful prediction* relating to some aspect of complex social behavior, whether it be smiling or tobacco buying. If these successful techniques exist outside of the reductive-functional approach, we need to examine them for consistency and generality. The question then becomes, "Can we ever predict behavior of this sort from a physiological and/or completely functional analysis?" My answer would take the form of the statements I made earlier concerning Winch's example of thinking according to causal sequence regarding Professor N. Logically, an analysis is possible involving a functional "causal" explanation underlying the cognitive activity about which we have made a prediction. It cannot be substituted for the cognitive analysis, however. It becomes another possible level of explanation dealing with the processes which lie behind the cognitive process, where the truth value (leading to better predictions) of either form is subject to the limitations discussed throughout this book.

In the criticism of the functional-reductive and conceptual positions, two points emerge. Science, in general, and psychology, in particular, must continue to explore problems in the functional-reductive manner, but the meaning attached to human activity is often impossible to explain by this approach. Because a good deal of successful reduction and functional explanation has already taken place in psychology, and because there is a compelling aspect to the parsimony of this approach, any complex phenomenon must be examined for the *possibility* of explaining it by reducing to a simpler level the elements or terms involved. However, if we do not recognize that meaning in social activity is quite often something different from functional relationships among observable variables, we are back to the point at which Hume found himself confused when he could find no necessity in the cause and effect relationship.

A conceptual-rational level of explanation of human phenomena is something in which most American psychologists have never really been interested (with some notable exceptions such as the gestalt psychologists transplanted from Germany, Koch [1956, 1964], and a few others). This has caused great confusion in their theorizing, especially within the context of social activity. The implications of continental ideas were always available to American psychologists, but they were never really taken seriously by them. Even the large acceptance of Freud in the United States took the form of embracing only the techniques and the more motivational aspects of psychoanalysis. Freud's interpretation of social activity has never really been very interesting to American social psychologists. And, as we have seen, Freud's theoretical position is very reductive in many ways, a characteristic which should have increased the probability of its assimilation by American psychologists.

A complete reductionist point of view (to the terms of physics) still necessitates taking a molar (nonreducible) position with respect to theorizing and empirical research, since one does not attain the ultimate base of the reduction immediately. Some theorists, having faith in reduction, go straight to physiology as a kind of reductive ultimate. I hope I have demonstrated this to be a position impossible to maintain as a means of understanding much of human activity.

Braithwaite suggests that in a functional system of explanation meaning is contained within the calculus and the deductive model, such that the deductive model is an interpretation of the calculus and may be used to explain a given set of empirical phenomena. This position may represent a rapprochement between the functional-reductive and conceptual-nonreductive approaches. The model need not be hypothetico-deductive in nature, but whatever its form meaning comes essentially from it (although Braithwaite might disagree with this interpretation). That is, the logical necessity for the validity of a system is contained therein. This may represent ultimate meaning and validity for a system of explanation, something which can never be provided by direct empirical reference. We refer here, of course, to causal statements only. Since most theories of explanation in psychology to date have been causal in nature, this suggestion is quite pertinent.

This book has not been an attempt to indicate what directions must be taken in social psychological research to attain successful prediction and explanation, but, rather, to indicate what assumptions, implicit and explicit, have been used by theorists and, therefore, what limitations exist in some modern approaches. It seems that we need to recognize these factors in order to proceed with meaningful research. The systems examined are fruitful for understanding many aspects of the social process. We have not always looked at their limitations in order to determine where they cannot take us in the future.

Marshall McLuhan and Social Psychology

Perhaps no one provides a better example of the meaningful overlap of experimental social psychology and artistic and historical efforts than Marshall McLuhan. A brief examination of some of his ideas that seem most pertinent to our discussion is a fitting envoi to the present study.

McLuhan is not a psychologist, nor are his ideas structured in a manner with which psychologists usually find themselves comfortable. His conclusions are not drawn from years of carefully controlled experimentation and cautious theorizing. Rather, they seem to be products of observing the development of society, and relating these observations to historical, literary, and scientific ideas of many kinds. McLuhan apparently takes seriously the idea that artists, writers, and historians, as well as scientists, possess a great deal of valid information about the nature of man's existence, information that is immediately useful for dealing with and understanding many of the problems confronted today by both individuals and nations.

McLuhan's major effort is *Understanding Media* (1965), which is designed to show the influence of developing technology on many of the processes of living, especially as this technology may be interpreted as information-providing media. The book is concerned with information transmission, and is directly related to the process of communication which, as we have seen, is also the concern of many of the theorists discussed in this book. McLuhan attempts no formal theory of communication, nor is his work an intellectual masterpiece of logically tight derivations following from given hypotheses. Rather, it is a series of loosely connected, remarkably perceptive and provocative observations about the way changes in technology have altered man and his habits over the course of human history.

While working in the area of persuasive communication for several years, I became increasingly aware of what I thought to be a curious fact about research in this area, including my own work. We were almost always concerned with aspects of the communicative situation which had little to do with the content, that is, with the empirical and logical aspects of the message that was being communicated. Most of us were interested in one or more of the following variables: the controversiality of the issue referred to in the communication, the awareness by the subject of the manipulatory intent of the communicator, the style used by the communicator, his prestige, the length of the communication, the medium used to transmit the communication (television, radio), and other variables of this type as well. In recent years, several researchers have turned toward the content and meaning of the communication (e.g., McGuire, 1960). However, much interest is still focused on factors which might be called "extrarational," in that they have nothing to do with the empirical and logical meaning of the persuasive message, or with its effect on the opinion or attitude of the subject. This research focus was not an accident of the interest patterns of the various psychologists doing work in communication. Of that I was convinced. Was it a natural by-product of American behaviorist tradition to focus on just about anything but meaning, or was something more fundamental operating? McLuhan provided a possible answer. As incredibly simple as it may seem in retrospect, psychologists were focusing on such things as the kind of medium used to convey the message, the style of the speaker, etc., because these very characteristics were messages in themselves. Prestige conveys information. A tape recorder conveys different information than does television, even though the empirical referents of the words and the logical structure of their arrangement are the same in both cases. This is true as well for the style and any manipulatory intent conveyed by the speaker. These all yield information different from the information conveyed by the ideas in the content of the message. This content is, in itself, another message providing other information. Psychologists were focused on appropriate sources of information, but they never really articulated reasons why they were doing so. It seems that McLuhan's contention provides a conceptually illuminating beginning for a re-examination of the process of persuasive communication.

Although McLuhan's book is fraught with difficulties and often confuses through contradiction, his perception of the process of communication is mostly astute and exciting. Most of the points that emerge from his discussion derive from his principal contention that technological change eventually creates a totally new human environment. This occurs because technological changes are extensions of ourselves, and necessitate new scales to judge the world around us. Thus, with the discovery of the wheel, the relations existing among human beings changed. Distance took on a different meaning. The speed of the distribution of goods changed. These facts, in turn, meant that it was no longer necessary for people to live close together in order to survive, which changed social patterns of interaction. The extension of the self, through some medium, is itself an instrument of change regardless of its content; it makes no difference what the wheel carried. The content of any medium is itself another medium. Speech acts as an influence independent of the actual content of thought which, in part, it reflects (McLuhan, 1965; Lana, 1963b). In today's world, electric media, culminating in the invention of television and computers, predominantly shape our world. For example, it will not avail the Oriental people to declare themselves spiritually and culturally antagonistic toward the social and cultural by-products of Western technology. So long as they accept the technology, they will also have the social and cultural changes, regardless of how they attempt to prevent them. The effects of technology do not occur on the conscious level of opinion or concept. Rather, without resistance on the part of the individual, they alter patterns of perception and, therefore, of behavior. McLuhan remarks that the only person capable of dealing with technology with impunity is the individual who is, or has the perception of, a serious artist, since he alone is aware of the changes in sense perception produced by the introduction of any new technology.

Many of the current pervasive technological developments of modern society have been dichotomized by McLuhan into "hot" and "cold." "Hot media" are those that extend one sense in "high definition," where the media themselves are well filled with data and therefore provide a minimum possibility for participation. On the other hand, "cold media" are not so well filled with data and allow for high participation. That is, it is possible for the recipient to complete the stimulus configuration by his own actions or thoughts. Examples of hot media are radio, motion pictures, still photographs, and lectures. Cold or "cool" media include television, telephone, cartoons, and seminars. McLuhan's arguments in support of choice of media to be placed in one category or the other are not always convincing. Indeed, in some cases, he does not provide any argument at all as to why a particular medium is hot or cool. For example, although one might see immediately why radio and television are placed in different categories, it is more difficult to understand why the motion picture is a low participational, hot medium. However, if there is any validity in this dichotomy, the implications are numerous for education, for television programming, as well as for many other modern societal functions.

McLuhan also characterizes cultures as "cool" or "hot" depending upon their general state of technological development. Primitive (tribal) non-literate cultures are cool, and this is reflected in their high participation in the functions of daily life. Also, they react rather violently to hot media such as the radio. Hot cultures such as most Western European nations and the United States (although it is changing) think of radio more as an entertainment medium and do not react to it so strongly. However, with the ascendance of the electric age which has produced, among other things, television, America is cooling off and becoming more tribal (in the same sense as a primitive society is tribal). Thus, cool media retribalizes modern man by bringing the world closer to him. Information coming from all parts of the world makes the world a "global village," and man returns to those considerations which are still found in primitive societies today. Washing machines, garbage disposal units, refrigerators, and the like, once again place the burden of preparing food, washing clothes, and so forth, on the individual, as they did and do in primitive societies. Only during the time when Western societies were at their "hottest" did these functions fall to menials, and the most favored in society were free from familial and tribal tasks of this sort.

There is one other principal idea of McLuhan's which I would like to introduce at this point. Hieroglyphic forms of writing, such as the Chinese ideogram, served to support the style of living in tribal, family-oriented societies. With the invention and use of the phonetic alphabet in the West, where semantically meaningless symbols were attached to semantically meaningless sounds, the tribal attachment was broken and "civilized man" was created. Separate individuals equal before a written code of law resulted from this technological change. The meaning of the symbols was unimportant. Patterns of visual uniformity and continuity were created by phonetic technology, thus extending man's visual function. Thought along linear dimensions, and therefore science, became possible. Sequence became all-important, rather than the perception of totalities, typical of primitive and tribal cultures. Linear causality was thus a by-product of the development of the phonetic alphabet. A specialist technology developed, where goods were produced by each individual's attending to a small part of the total product, constructing it piece by piece in a linear fashion, such as in an assembly line. The specialist function served to change the social patterns of society. In modern times, specialization is less and less useful. The computer, for example, can accomplish more efficiently those functions formerly performed by many specialists. Nonspecific electric technologies retribalize man in that it is again necessary to perceive total processes. A man must program a computer with all elements of the job to be done in mind. McLuhan describes an experiment which indicates the empirical research possibilities derivable from his interpretation of the effects of communication media on behavior.

In a group of simulcasts of several media done in Toronto a few years back, TV did a strange flip. Four randomized groups of university students were given the same information at the same time about the structure of preliterate languages. One group received it via radio, one from TV, one by lecture, and one read it. For all but the reader group, the information was passed along in straight verbal flow by the same speaker without discussion or questions or use of blackboard. Each group had half an hour of exposure to the material. Each was asked to fill in the same quiz afterward. It was quite a surprise to the experimenters when the students performed better with TV-channeled information and with radio than with lecture and print—and the TV group stood *well* above the radio group. Since nothing had been done to give special stress to any of these four media, the experiment was repeated with other randomized groups. This time each medium was allowed full opportunity to do its stuff. For radio and TV, the material was dramatized with many auditory and visual features. The lecturer took full advantage of the blackboard and class discussion. The printed form was embellished with an imaginative use of typography and page layout to stress each point in the lecture. All of these media had been stepped up to high intensity for this repeat of the original performance. Television and radio once again showed results high above lecture and print. Unexpectedly to the testers, however, radio now stood significantly above television. It was a long time before the obvious reason declared itself, namely that TV is a cool, participant medium. When hotted up by dramatization and stingers, it performs less well because there is less opportunity for participation. Radio is a hot medium. When given additional intensity, it performs better. It doesn't invite the same degree of participation in its users. Radio will serve as background-sound or as noise-level control, as when the ingenious teenager employs it as a means of privacy. TV will not work as background. It engages you. You have to be *with* it. (The phrase has gained acceptance since TV.)[1]

In this brief summary of some of McLuhan's major ideas, we have tried to indicate the kind of approach that is possible without benefit of the experimental method or of the careful, logical techniques of a scientific theoretician. His ideas are provocative and insightful. They provide a number of ideas which possibly can be tested within the framework of experimental and theoretical modes of thinking. McLuhan's techniques lie somewhere near the convergence of literature, history, and science. They convince the present author, at least, that these areas are more related for *practical purposes* than many psychologists may be willing to concede.

[1] From UNDERSTANDING MEDIA: The Extensions of Man by Marshall McLuhan. Used by permission of McGraw-Hill Book Company.

References

Anderson, N. H. Test of a model for opinion change. *J. abn. soc. Psychol.*, 1959, **59**, 371-381.

Aristotle. *The works of Aristotle.* (Transl. R. P. Hardie and R. K. Gaze), Vol. II. *Physica.* London: Oxford of the Clarendon Press, 1930.

Asch, S. E., *Social psychology.* Englewood Cliffs, New Jersey: Prentice-Hall, 1952.

Bandura, A. & Walters, R. H. *Social learning and personality development.* New York: Holt, Rinehart, and Winston, 1963.

Boring, E. *A history of experimental psychology.* (2nd ed.) New York: Appleton-Century-Crofts, 1950.

Braithwaite, R. B. *Scientific exploration.* New York: Harper, 1960.

Bunge, M. *Causality.* Cambridge, Mass.: Harvard Univer. Press, 1959.

Chapanis, N. P. & Chapanis, A. Cognitive dissonance: Five years later. *Psychol. Bull.,* 1964, **61**, 1-22.

Chomsky, N. A review of B. F. Skinner's verbal behavior. In *Language.* New York: Appleton-Century-Crofts, 1959, **35**, 26-58.

Dollard, J., & Miller, N. E. *Personality and psychotherapy.* New York: McGraw-Hill, 1950.

Dostoyevsky, F. *Notes from underground.* (Transl. Andrew R. McAndrew) New York: The New American Library, 1961.

Entwisle, Doris R. Attensity: Factors of specific set on school learning. *Harvard Educational Rev.,* 1961, **31**, 84-101. (a)

Entwisle, D. R. Interaction effects on pretesting. *Psychol. Educ. Measmt.,* 1961, **21**, 607-620. (b)

Festinger, L. *A theory of cognitive dissonance.* Stanford, California: Stanford Univer. Press, 1957.

Fiedler, F. E. A contingency model of leadership effectiveness. Unpublished paper based on Fiedler, F. E., Osgood, C. E., Stolurow, L. M., & Triacles, H. C., Group and organizational factors influencing creativity. *Technical Report* #10, ONR Project NR-177-472, Wonr 1834 (36) July, 1963.

Freud, S. *The ego and the id.* (Transl. Joan Riviere & James Strachey) New York: W. W. Norton Co., 1960.

Freud, S. *Group psychology and the analysis of the ego.* (Transl. James Strachey) New York: Bantam Books, 1960.

Galileo, *Dialogo sopra i due massimi sistemi del mondo* In *Opere*. Vol. 7, Edizione Nazionale (Florence, 1890-1909).

Helson, H. *Adaptation level theory.* New York: Harper & Row, 1964.

Hogben, L. *Statistical theory.* London: George Allen and Unwin Ltd., 1957.

Horney, Karen. *The neurotic personality of our time.* New York: W. W. Norton Co., 1937.

Horney, Karen. *New ways in psychoanalysis.* New York: W. W. Norton Co., 1939.

Hovland, C. I., Janis L., & Kelley, Harold H. *Communication and persuasion.* New Haven, Conn.: Yale Univer. Press, 1953.

Hovland, C. I. (Ed.) *The order of presentation in persuasion.* New Haven, Conn.: Yale Univer. Press, 1957.

Hull, C. L. *Principles of behavior.* New York: Appleton-Century-Crofts, 1943.

Hume, D. *A treatise of human nature.* Garden City, New York: Doubleday, 1961.

Jessor, R. The problem of reductionism in psychology. *Psychol. Rev.,* 1958, **65,** 170-178.

Kant, I. *Critique of pure reason.* (2nd ed.) Garden City, New York: Doubleday, 1961.

Koch, S. Behavior as "intrinsically" regulated: Work notes towards a pre-theory of phenomena called "motivational." In Jones, M. (Ed.), *Nebraska symposium on motivation.* Lincoln, Nebraska: Univer. Nebraska Press, 1956.

Koch, S. Psychology and emerging conceptions of knowledge as unitary. In Wann, T. W. (Ed.) *Behaviorism and phenomenology,* Chicago: Univer. Chicago Press, 1964.

Koffka, K. *Principles of gestalt psychology*. New York: Harcourt, Brace, 1935.

Krech, D., & Crutchfield, R. S. *Theory and problems of social psychology*. New York: McGraw-Hill, 1948.

Lana, R. E. A further investigation of the pretest-treatment interaction effect. *J. appl. Psychol.*, 1959, **43**, 421-422. (a)

Lana, R. E. Pretest-treatment interaction effects in attitudinal studies. *Psychol. Bull.*, 1959, **56**, 293-300. (b)

Lana, R. E. Familiarity and the order of presentation of persuasive communications. *J. abn. soc. Psychol.*, 1961, **62**, 573-577.

Lana, R. E. Controversy of the topic and the order of presentation in persuasive communications. *Psychol. Reps.*, 1963, **12**, 163-170. (a)

Lana, R. E. Interest, media, and order effects in persuasive communications. *J. Psychol.*, 1963, **56**, 9-13. (b)

Lana, R. E. Existing familiarity and order of presentation of persuasive communications. *Psychol. Reps.*, 1964, **15**, 607-610. (a)

Lana, R. E. The influence of the pretest on order effects in persuasive communications. *J. abn. soc. Psychol.*, 1964, **69**, 337-341. (b)

Lana, R. E. Three theoretical interpretations of order effects in persuasive communications. *Psychol. Bull.*, 1964, **61**, 314-320. (c)

Lana, R. E. Inhibitory effects of a pretest on opinion change. *Educ. Psychol. Measmt.*, 1966, **26**, 139-150.

Lana, R. E. Pretest sensitization. In Rosenthal, R., & Rosnow, R. (Eds.), *Artifact in behavioral research*. New York: Academic Press, in press.

Lana, R. E., & King, D. J. Learning factors as determiners of pretest sensitization. *J. appl. Psychol.*, 1960, **44**, 189-191.

Lana, R. E., & Lubin, A. The effect of correlation on the repeated measures design. *Educ. Psychol. Measmt.*, 1963, **23**, 729-739.

Lana, R. E., & Rosnow, R. L. Subject awareness and order effects in persuasive communications. *Psychol. Reps.*, 1963, **12**, 523-529.

Lewin, K. *A dynamic theory of personality*. New York: McGraw-Hill, 1935.

Lorenz, K. *On aggression*. New York: Harcourt, Brace & World, 1963.

McDougall, W. *An introduction to social psychology*. London: Methuen, 1960.

Mach, E. *The analysis of sensation*. New York: Dover, 1959.

McGuire, W. J., A syllogistic analysis of cognitive relationship. In Rosenberg, M. J., et al., *Attitude organization and change.* New Haven, Conn.: Yale Univer. Press, 1960.

Mahler, W. *Ersatzhandlungen verscheidener Resalitätsgrades Psych. Forsch.* 1933, **18,** 27-89. Reported in Lewin, K. *A dynamic theory of personality.* New York: McGraw-Hill, 1935.

McLuhan, M. *Understanding media: The extension of man.* New York: McGraw-Hill, 1965.

Miller, G. A. Some preliminaries to psycholinguistics. *Amer. Psychology,* 1965, **20,** 15-20.

Molnar, A. The effects of styles, speakers and arguments on the attitudes and perceptions of a listening audience. Unpublished master's thesis, University of Maryland, 1955.

Monroe, Ruth L. *Schools of psychoanalytic thought.* New York: Dryden Press, 1955.

Newcomb, T. M. *Social psychology.* New York: Dryden Press, 1950.

Newcomb, T. M., Turner, R. H., & Converse, Philip E. *Social psychology: The study of human interaction.* New York: Holt, Rinehart and Winston, 1965.

Nissen, H. The nature of the drive as innate determiner of behavioral organization. In Jones, M. (Ed.), *Nebraska symposium on motivation 1954.* Lincoln, Nebraska: Univer. of Nebraska Press.

Pap, A. *An introduction to the philosophy of science.* Glencoe, Ill.: Free Press, 1962.

Peters, R. S. *The concept of motivation.* New York: Humanities Press, 1958.

Rosnow, R. L., & Lana, R. E. Complementary and competing-order effects in opinion change. *J. soc. Psychol.,* 1965, **66,** 201-207.

Rosnow, R. L., & Russell, G. Spread of effect of reinforcement in persuasive communications. *Psychol. Reps.,* 1963, **12,** 731-735.

Russell, B. *Our knowledge of the external world.* New York: The New American Library, 1960.

Russell, B. *Human knowledge, its scope and limits.* New York: Simon and Schuster, 1962.

Schramm, W. Mass communication. In *Annual review of psychology,* 1962, **13,** Palo Alto, California: Annual Rev. Inc.

References 173

Schultz, D. P. Primacy-recency within a sensory variation framework. *Psychol. Rec.*, 1963, **13,** 129-139. (a)

Schultz, D. P. Time, awareness, and order of presentation in opinion change. *J. appl. Psychol.*, 1963, **47,** 280-283. (b)

Sherif, Carolyn W., Sherif, M., & Nebergall, R. E. *Attitude and attitude change.* Philadelphia: W. B. Saunders, 1965.

Sidman, M. *Tactics of Scientific Research.* New York: Basic Books, Inc. Publishers, 1960.

Skinner, B. F. *Walden II.* New York: Macmillan, 1948.

Skinner, B. F. *Science and human behavior.* New York: Macmillan, 1953.

Skinner, B. F. *Verbal behavior.* New York: Appleton-Century-Crofts, 1957.

Solomon, R. L. An extension of control group design. *Psychol. Bull.*, 1949, **46,** 137-150.

Steiner, I. D. Group dynamics. In *Annual review of psychology,* 1964, **15,** Palo Alto, California: Annual Revs. Inc.

Thomas, E. J., Webb, S., & Tweedie, J. Effects of familiarity with a controversial issue on acceptance of successive persuasive communications. *J. abn. soc. Psychol.*, 1961, **63,** 636-659.

Winch, P. *The idea of a social science.* New York: Humanities Press, 1958.

Winer, B. J. *Statistical principles in experimental design.* New York: McGraw-Hill, 1962.

Zeigarnik, B. *Über das Behalten erledigter und unerledigter Handlungen. Psych. Forsch.*, 1927, **9,** 1-85. Reported in Lewin, K. *A dynamic theory of personality.* New York: McGraw-Hill, 1935.

Index